Fright to the Point

Fright to the Point

Ghosts of West Point

13 Tales of the Supernatural from the
United States Military Academy at West Point

Major Thad Krasnesky

Schiffer Publishing Ltd

4880 Lower Valley Road, Atglen, Pennsylvania 19310

Dedication

This book is dedicated to my father, Henry Krasnesky, who passed away shortly after the book was completed. He first piqued my interest in the paranormal when I was a child by regaling me with stories of our own family ghosts. Although I am still somewhat a skeptic myself, Dad, if you want to drop by and say "Hi," sometime I would welcome it. I love you.

Schiffer Books are available at special discounts for bulk purchases for sales promotions or premiums. Special editions, including personalized covers, corporate imprints, and excerpts can be created in large quantities for special needs. For more information contact the publisher:

Published by Schiffer Publishing Ltd.
4880 Lower Valley Road
Atglen, PA 19310
Phone: (610) 593-1777; Fax: (610) 593-2002
E-mail: Info@schifferbooks.com

For the largest selection of fine reference books on this and related subjects,
please visit our website at
www.schifferbooks.com
We are always looking for people to write books on new and related subjects.
If you have an idea for a book, please contact us at
proposals@schifferbooks.com

This book may be purchased from the publisher.
Include $5.00 for shipping.
Please try your bookstore first.
You may write for a free catalog.

In Europe, Schiffer books are distributed by
Bushwood Books
6 Marksbury Ave.
Kew Gardens
Surrey TW9 4JF England
Phone: 44 (0) 20 8392 8585; Fax: 44 (0) 20 8392 9876
E-mail: info@bushwoodbooks.co.uk
Website: www.bushwoodbooks.co.uk

Designed by Mark David Bowyer
Type set in Rosemary Roman / NewBaskerville BT

ISBN: 978-0-7643-3918-9
Printed in the United States of America

Contents

Acknowledgments

There are many people who I would like to thank that helped make this book possible. First of all, I would like to thank Colonel Lance Betros who is the head of the History department at West Point. He was the one who first introduced me to the specters that lurk behind West Point's walls. I would like to thank Dr. Stephen Groves, former West Point Historian for thirty years who read through the manuscript and gave me many helpful editorial comments. I would also like to thank Dr. Sherman Fleek, current West Point Historian and author of several well-regarded books. Sherman allowed me access to many seldom-seen archives at West Point, and in the process, wound up becoming a very good friend. My wife and daughters were also very helpful, serving as literary guinea pigs as they read through the stories. And of course it goes without saying that a large thanks goes to the United States Military Academy itself. I appreciate the opportunity that West Point gave me to look beyond the public icon of the sterling fortress on the hill and see the darker image that lies beneath. A portion of the proceeds from this book will be dedicated to the West Point Museum.

Foreword

I am a skeptic. That may seem like an odd admission from someone who has just written a book on ghost stories but I think that it is important that you understand the process behind the creation of this work. I would offer that perhaps I should be considered an optimistic skeptic. Or maybe a supernatural agnostic would be a better term. Like the picture behind David Duchovny's character in *The X-Files* reads, "I want to believe." There are times that I want to believe in such things as bigfoot or the Loch Ness monster or aliens. Or ghosts. I consider myself a rational adult but there is always this nagging whisper of "What if…?" echoing around the back of my head. No matter what I have read or heard or seen however, once the sun has risen and the shadows are dispersed, I find (some might say, "create") explanations for the unexplainable and am unable to fully commit my belief.

It was from this position that I first became acquainted with the "shadow residents" of The Point. Stories from professors told as humorous examples of folkloric history lead to several interviews with cadets and former cadets. These stories often ended with lines such as, "…but of course it couldn't really have been a ghost." This is the way that society dictates that we end such stories. The sunlit world of rationalism constrains us to avow our disbelief of what we have personally seen and experienced. And yet whatever disclaimers came out of the mouths of those who had personally experienced these stories, the belief, and sometimes fear, in their eyes spoke louder than their words.

That is how I began my research into these stories. I told myself that I was merely interested in oral history and the psychology behind the folkloric tales. That is what we, as skeptics, must tell ourselves any time we venture down such a path. Because that path has been traveled too often by those who then find themselves lost among the byways and hedgerows that serve as the tenuous boundaries between what is real and what is illusory. We skeptics tell ourselves it can't be real. We vow to ignore the shapes that lope along the path beside us, always just out of sight. That is the only way that we feel safe. That is the only way that we know that we can return.

So if you find yourself getting too far along that path and feel in fear of getting lost, tell yourself that these are only stories. It is what I do. It is what all skeptics do if we wish to sleep soundly through the night. Sometimes it even works.

~Major Thad Krasnesky

1

The Dark Bride of Morrison House

There are many benefits to being the spouse of a military officer. The pay is not insignificant, the benefits are many, the housing (at least in the past) is commensurate with the rank, and there is a certain amount of prestige associated with the profession. For most spouses, it is simply a matter of happenstance, but for many it is a goal. And to one or two, the title of officer's wife is something worth killing for. Such is the case of the antagonist of our first tale.

In the period following the Civil War, the western territories were wide open. There were vast expanses that held more buffalo and prairie dogs than people. Miles and miles of open plains and mountain ranges would seem to go on endlessly before they encountered even a token town or settlement. Among these vast open spaces even the nomadic settlements of the native peoples were nothing more than a pin prick on a canvas.

Into this barrenness, the federal government injected small outposts of soldiers. Ostensibly this was to help keep the peace in areas that lacked any form of constabulary, but in fact this was the beginning of a series of forts that would be used to fight, control, and eventually eliminate the Native Americans from most areas. One of these nominal forts was established on the edge of a mining area in the Dakotas. The local settlement was rough in nature and in character. Shops were little more than squared-off rooms stacked with goods, lacking any formal counters or display shelves. Saloons, and there were many of them, had no fancy wooden bars with expensive mirrors or paintings hanging behind them.

Morrison House. It stands on the corner of Washington Avenue and Stony Lonesome. It is the last in a row of houses known as Professor's Row. Since the tragedies that occurred there over 130 years ago, the house has gone through several series of renovations.

They were nothing more than a rough plank set across empty crates or barrels that served only one type of liquor that probably did not even qualify to be called whiskey. The people were no different. They had only enough clothing to allow one set to be cleaned or repaired while the other was being worn.

Everything was functional and the word fashion was not even a concept. There were no schools or churches in the area. At the time of the story there were not even any barber shops. Hair and beards were simply allowed to grow and if it got long enough to be an annoyance you just grabbed up a handful of it and cut it with a knife. Any other type of hygiene was purely optional.

There was one exception to this rule. A farmer who was eking out a living by growing his stunted crop in the weak soil and selling the surplus to the miners and drovers had a daughter who was named Vivian. Vivian was noticeably different from the time she was little. Her eyes were more than just clear, they had a spark to them. Her teeth came in straight and clean. Her skin defied the rough weather and rough life of the Dakotas and remained as soft and smooth and flawless as the day she was born. Her hair shone like the gold that the men toiled for in vain. And as she grew, her figure did not become the one size fits all that most of the pioneer women of that area tended towards, but instead blossomed into a distinct shape of its own that had not been seen by most of those around in ages. She was beautiful. Considering the circumstances, it might be easier to simply dismiss tales of her beauty and say that by comparison, anyone of even average looks would have been held in high esteem by those used to the stout, cowish women of that town, but that simply was not the case. Vivian would have been beautiful in any town, in any era.

On top of her looks, Vivian also had an intellect. She was not satisfied to simply learn the skills of housekeeping and child-rearing and get married to the first promising prospector or farmer that came along. She sought to better herself and learn things. This was a difficult task in a town that had no formal school but Vivian managed to do it. By the age of seven, this daughter of an illiterate farmer had somehow managed to teach herself to read and write and soon managed to locate and read every book that the small town held.

She developed a sense of self, an individuality that was evidenced in the way that she spoke, the way that she walked, and the way that she dressed. Although she wore the same fabrics that everyone else in town wore, she made her dresses herself and somehow the simple shifts that everyone else draped around themselves did not seem to sit the same on the shapely form of Vivian.

Although she had not managed to acquire makeup, if such a thing existed in this little backwater, she really needed none. She practiced normal hygiene and her natural beauty did the rest. Vivian began to have a singular effect on all of those around her. It was almost as if everyone had forgotten what beauty was, and now that Vivian had reminded them of it, they wanted a piece of it for themselves. Shops began to actually sweep their floors and discourage customers from spitting on or around the merchandise. One of the saloons in town bought a mirror, a small one, and began washing their glasses. A farmer left his barren plot of land and went into business as a barber and people actually came to him. There was even talk of hiring a schoolmaster and letting him use the empty livery building as a school to teach the kids a little bit of math and reading.

In the grand scheme of things, Vivian had the potential to be one of those wonderful change agents and make a difference in many lives, had it not been for one thing. Along with her looks and intelligence and individuality, Vivian had ambition. Not a quiet, good-natured ambition, but an overwhelming driving force that had not had the benefit of being tempered by a church, since there weren't any in the area, nor tempered by normal social constraints, since social constructs were alien to this little town. She wanted what she wanted and she had the skills to get it. And what Vivian wanted most was to get out of that small town.

Marriage...A Means to an End?

This is where the fort comes into the picture. Vivian had no end to her list of suitors. By the time she was 13, men were lining up to bribe, threaten, and cajole her father into giving them her hand in marriage. Vivian had as much control over her father as she had on everything though and none of the rough men of the area would do for her. She saw the soldiers of the nearby fort as much more suitable mates. In her mind, they were a conduit to an outside world that she longed to join. It was not long then before she found a young and attractive cavalry soldier who was more than happy to spend time with her, and by the time she was 15, a marriage had been arranged.

Initially Vivian was ecstatic about her new prospects, but a year later, when she found herself still living in the same little town, her outlook soured. She was bright but her education was extremely limited. She had not realized that the soldiers at the fort might wind up being stationed at the same little outpost for four or five years at a time, possibly even longer. She also quickly became soured on her new husband. In contrast to the local crop of men, he was certainly clean cut and attractive, but he lacked a stimulating level of intelligence for Vivian. He also lacked her ambition.

Vivian used her new connections at the fort to continue her education. She expanded the number of books to which she had access and quickly learned the ropes of the military. She soon determined that if she wanted to really get out of the area and have all of those things she desired, she needed to be a colonel's wife. The downside of that was that there were only two routes to becoming a colonel's wife in that tiny outpost. The first was to marry one of the small number of lieutenants or possibly captains at the post and then wait patiently for twenty years and hope they got promoted up through the ranks. The second was to marry an existing colonel, but there was only one of them and he was already married. Either one of these options was also already hampered by the fact that she was currently married.

Vivian, however, was nothing if not ambitious. She did not plan on letting little things like marriage get in her way. It was a serendipitous turn of events then (for Vivian, not for her husband) that her husband went riding one day with her and happened to be attacked by a renegade band of "Indians." The "Indians" somehow wound up beheading the young cavalry soldier but decided to show mercy to the young Vivian and left her unharmed. There were of course some unkind souls in the area that questioned why the native tribes would have beheaded the young man since that was not a common practice. Some even questioned where the "rogue" tribe came from since there had not been any problems with them in the history of the fort. Overall though, most of the residents of the town and the fort felt sorry for the young widow and mourned with her. The period of mourning was barely over when the not quite 18-year-old Vivian found the attention of a young officer at the post. An appropriate time was set for the courtship and then the young girl found herself a bride for the second time.

As the bride of an officer, Vivian found her position immeasurably improved but was still not satisfied. She continued her education, quickly making friends with the commanding officer's wife and learning everything that a young officer's wife needed to know. Unfortunately, one of the things that she learned was that even though she saw the officers come and go with more frequency than she did the enlisted soldiers, it did not necessarily mean that they were going anywhere that she had a desire to go. In order to get promotions, it was often necessary that the officer "do his time" and serve in a variety of small western outposts.

So Vivian found herself moving from her small, insignificant town in the Dakotas to a fort near a small, insignificant town in the Wyoming territory that was even further away from the culture of the east that she so much longed for. This did not sit well with the young bride. Fortune once again smiled on her, however, in the form of a young captain with orders heading back east and yet another band of "rogue Indians." In a disturbingly strange coincidence, her second husband was attacked and beheaded by a band of Indians while she was again left unharmed. Had anyone at the new fort been present or familiar with the circumstances of the death of her first husband, this might have raised a few eyebrows but the natives were often the boogeymen of any unsolved crime and no one questioned her retelling of the incident. Since the captain had immediate orders to return east, there was no time for a proper mourning. The local population was scandalized by the immediate remarriage of the young widow, but since Vivian was leaving she did not care too much that she had upset anyone's sensitivities.

It was at this time that Vivian came to West Point. The young cavalry officer had been assigned to assist the cadets at the academy with their riding skills. Now suddenly the flood gates of knowledge were opened up to Vivian. She was living on a university campus and had no limit to her access to books. For the first two years it was the happiest time of her life. She was completely occupied by social events at the Point and making trips into New York City. The fashions and the customs were an endless source of wonder for her. And when she was not involved in a social activity, she could be found sitting in her favorite chair reading an unending stream of books. It was also rumored (unkindly and as an after-note) that the 18- and 19-year-old Vivian found the time to be "tutored" by many of the young cadets. This, however, is not very likely since ambition was her driving characteristic and it was unlikely that she would have spent her time with a cadet who would not have benefited her in the long run. Jealousy makes such stories common, however, when someone is as beautiful as Vivian was.

Had circumstances remained unchanged, it is possible that Vivian would have remained in her halcyon state. Circumstances, however, rarely remain unchanged. At the end of two years, the cavalry captain received orders to change duty stations and leave West Point.

This was not something that Vivian could tolerate. She could not fathom returning to the lifestyle that she had so assiduously spurned. The frontier held no adventure for her as it did for some. She had already lived that life. Life beyond the Ohio River, for Vivian, held only the terror of the mundane.

What happened next should come as no surprise to those that know all of the details of Vivian's life. "Thieves" broke into the house one evening and robbed the young couple. As you may have guessed, the "thieves" wound up beheading the cavalry captain while deciding to bestow mercy upon the young woman and leave her unharmed. This was quite the heinous crime. Being far from the lawless frontier, an investigation was launched into what was a rather high-profile crime. Try as they might, however, the investigators were unable to turn up any clues as to the identities of the killers.

Once again another year passed while Vivian sat in mourning. She was now thrice a widow although most people were only aware of the last husband with only a handful having any knowledge of either of the first two unlucky gentlemen. At not quite 21 years old, most people would have simply called it quits at that point and determined that perhaps marriage was not for her. Vivian, however, would not stand for it. After the passing of the official period of mourning, it was not long before Vivian used her connections at West Point to make the acquaintance of an older colonel who was a professor at West Point and a widower himself. It did not seem too unlikely to the casual observer that the still-beautiful young widow and the educated older widower would find common grounds in their bereavement and eventually develop a relationship. An engagement was announced and soon afterwards the wedding was celebrated.

Being a full professor, the colonel had a fine house on professor's row on Washington Avenue at West Point. It was the Morrison House that sits at the corner of Stony Lonesome and Washington Avenue. It was not likely that a poor daughter of a backwater frontier town could have been expected to do any better in those days. By all accounts, Vivian once again seemed to be fully comfortable in her social position and new role as a colonel's wife. She lived in the nicest house that she had ever known, she had access to more money than she had ever known, and she moved in the best of social circles. Vivian entertained her professor husband for hours on end by sitting and listening enraptured as he would teach her just as he would one of his students. Several years passed without the need for any Indians or thieves to attack any more husbands.

No good thing lasts forever though. After living in the Morrison House for five years, the professor was considering retiring. He had been there already for seven years at the time he had gotten married, and now after twelve years teaching was ready to move on. Vivian, however, was not. It is possible that Vivian might have actually developed an emotional attachment to this last husband, however, since thieves did not strike immediately. Instead they had many heated and lengthy discussions regarding the pros and cons of remaining at the academy. This extended their time there by another year but in the end, age and the military forced the older man to offer his retirement papers.

Vivian was only 27 years old at the time. She was not ready to move on. It was a sad predictable fate then that one morning the police were called to the Morrison House and Vivian practiced her well-rehearsed story of a break in, violent thieves, and a husband who was now very much without a head. There was not enough time or distance between this incident and the earlier one at the point involving the young cavalry captain. The similarities were too graphic. The investigators did not take long to put a case together. As the investigation continued, they even uncovered evidence of the beheaded lieutenant and the very first unfortunate young enlisted cavalry soldier who had fallen under the spell of the then 15-year-old femme fatale. It was not long before the indictment of murder was handed down.

Vivian still had that beauty and charm, however, that disarmed most who came into contact with her. Whereas most people would have been brought into custody almost immediately, Vivian was allowed to remain in the Morrison House until the evidence gave them no choice but to bring her in. It was with a fair degree of reluctance that the local Marshall and the military police officer made their way to arrest Vivian. Vivian was still adamant in her refusal not to leave the home to which she had become accustomed. When the officials arrived at the home, their knocks were met with ominous silence. After an uncomfortable moment on the door step, they finally proceeded to enter the home.

What they found in the front parlor was almost as gruesome as the scene that they had found on the morning of the murder. The beautiful young Vivian was lying on the floor in a pool of blood. Saying that she was lying face down would have been a misnomer. She was indeed lying on her stomach so that under normal circumstances her face would have been towards the floor but instead, the grotesquely pale face was turned around and staring up at them as if she were looking over her shoulder. This was made possible due to the fact that her head had been almost, but not completely, severed from her neck. The implement used to exact this brutal montage was a wickedly shiny and sharp hatchet that was held in Vivian's hand.

Vivian's death was ruled a suicide. No one could quite explain how someone had wielded a hatchet in such a brutal manner upon themselves but there were so many other questions that remained unanswered that this one hardly mattered. Why did this beautiful young girl feel the need to act out in such a violent manner? Why did such an intelligent girl murder people in the same way over and over again? Was someone that was capable of picking up Latin and Greek not aware that beheading people was a memorable act that would eventually be found out? What was the dark force that drove this young girl who on the exterior was so full of light?

The Haunting...

Those questions perhaps began to be answered shortly after the murder and suicide. Strange sounds and lights were heard and seen coming from the Morrison House. When investigated, there never appeared to be anyone or anything there. After the house was cleaned up and a suitable time had passed, the house was occupied once again. Another professor took ownership of the home and settled into his academic life at the point. The strange sounds and sights did not cease after the occupation. The most common complaints were rather generic complaints of moans and creaks and severely cold spots that seemed to come and go. Those who did not experience these incidents firsthand put them aside as nothing more than the normal creaks and drafts that any old house has. Guests and residents, however knew differently. Creaks do not sound like screams and drafts do not feel like a cold, thick liquid has just been poured down your leg.

One of the more graphic and well-known incidents occurred with the third resident following the murder and just prior to the turn of the century. The professor that lived in the home had a wife and three small children. Upon arriving home late one evening after a particularly long day, the professor was startled to find a large pool of blood on the floor in his front parlor. Fearing the worst, but seeing no one around, he immediately began rushing around the house in search of his wife and children. Racing up the stairs he found his wife on the bed. At first he thought that she was dead. She did not seem to be breathing and she was completely unresponsive to his touch or his call. He dashed out of the house to find help. The neighbor in the next house over was immediately roused and entered the home to help. They testified that there was indeed a large pool of blood in the parlor. A continued search of the house turned up the unresponsive woman upstairs but no sign of the children. A general alarm was put out and immediately military police and neighbors rushed over.

As the first group of responders crossed the threshold, confusion set in. None of the later visitors reported seeing any sign of blood in the parlor. The professor's wife descended down the stairs and was quite

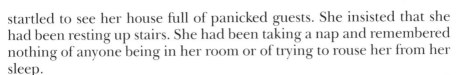

startled to see her house full of panicked guests. She insisted that she had been resting up stairs. She had been taking a nap and remembered nothing of anyone being in her room or of trying to rouse her from her sleep.

The children suddenly appeared from seemingly nowhere and had the strangest story of all to tell. They had come down the stairs that afternoon and had seen the huge pool of blood. Immediately, they had tried to alert their mother about it but had been prevented from leaving the room. They had tried going out the front door and the side door, but it was as if they were being held back by large pillows that they could not push through. They had panicked and shouted out but no one had seemed to hear them. They reported that they had been in the parlor the entire time and had seen everything going on. They said that everyone had passed right by them and even through them. They had shouted out and tried to contact the people rushing by but it was as if they had been speaking through water. They don't know why they were suddenly released but they could feel a physical force pass through them and suddenly they were able to be seen and heard again.

No one could explain how or why it happened. It was more than just weird lights and sounds though and was more difficult to simply dismiss as the normal sounds of a house settling.

This incident was compounded a few years later when the next resident of the home had a more mundane occurrence but one that was almost just as disturbing. The elderly professor, who was in residence in the house at the time, lived there with his wife. His children were already grown and were no longer living at home. One morning the professor awoke to find his wife standing over him and screaming as she dashed a hatchet at his head again and again. He barely dared to move as the hatchet descended again and again. He recalled hearing his wife screaming over and over again, "No! No! Stop it!" He finally managed to roll to the side and get off of the opposite side of the bed. His wife, however, had not moved and continued to dash the hatchet at the space where he had been. The professor sensed that his wife was in distress and despite the danger rushed over to her side. He grabbed the hand with the hatchet and almost immediately his wife went limp and fell to the floor. He placed the hatchet down on the night stand and laid his wife out on the bed.

She rapidly regained consciousness and immediately began crying and begging his forgiveness. She said that she could not remember how she had gotten there or where the hatchet had come from. She said that it felt as though someone else were controlling her body. It had taken all of her energy and strength to keep this other force from slashing the hatchet into her husband's neck. The husband did not know what to make of the story. There was no reason to think that his wife would have wanted him dead and if she really had, she certainly would have been able to do it before he awoke. He also was familiar with many of the strange incidents that had already occurred to them in the house and had heard rumors about the incident that had happened to the resident before him. As if to seal the event, when he turned to take the hatchet from the night stand and examine it, it was nowhere to be found.

The professor immediately moved out and the house remained vacant for the next twenty years.

Faded Memories

Eventually, memories faded, and after extensive renovations, the house was once again reoccupied. It was almost as if the house took time to rebuild its energy, but soon, the strange lights and sounds began to be reported again. The occurrences peaked once again with an incident about which little is known. The end result was that one evening, two of the younger daughters of the professor who occupied the house at the time went screaming out into the night, clad only in the glow of the full moon above. The spectacle brought out several neighbors who attempted to calm down and cover up the two hysterical girls. This was not only awkward but proved to be impossible. Eventually, the two nude girls fled across the street and up the stairs to the Catholic Chapel on the hill next to them. It was inside the church that the parish priest was finally able to calm them and cast some vestments about them.

Neither of the girls ever spoke of what it was that had sent them screaming out into the night nor why it was that they were without clothes. This brought about a second extended period of time during which the home was "closed for renovation." It was not until the late sixties that it was finally opened again. Once again the stories continued. Whatever renovations were being conducted did not seem capable of altering whatever had been imprinted upon the home when Vivian had murdered the professor and then had taken her own life afterwards. Walls could be removed and appliances replaced. Chimneys bricked over and floors refinished. No amount of carpentry or masonry seems likely to ever be able to remove the spirit of Vivian from the house that she took such dastardly steps to remain in and now seems attached to it for all eternity.

You are of course welcome to stop by Morrison House at any time and ask the current residents if they have had any strange encounters there. That is, you would be if there were any residents currently staying there. Sadly though, it seems that it is under renovation.

2
Two For the Price of One

The superintendent's house at West Point is the second oldest surviving structure at the academy. It dates back to 1819, with portions of the house possibly predating even that. It has been continuously occupied since its completion, minus a few periods of renovation and expansion, and has housed every academy superintendent since it was constructed. In addition to serving as a residence, classes were even held there during the earlier years and tutoring sessions were conducted in it well into the twentieth century. Even today it is still used to host formal functions. It comprises well over 7,000 square feet and has housed distinguished visitors from all around the world. During football season, its extensive and well maintained gardens host spirit rallies prior to each game. It is the spirits of another world, however, and not those of school pride, that often take center-stage at the residence.

It is not surprising that a house that is so old and has such an illustrious past would be home to an extensive collection of spirits. An entire volume could probably be composed dealing with just those entities that reside in the superintendent's house, however, since this is intended to be a book of ghost stories from all around the Point, we will pick just one of those stories. We will cheat though and choose a story that has two distinct spirits associated with it. One story with two spirits; the first one, a resident of the home, and the second, a traveling spirit that spends her time moving back and forth between the superintendent's house and the kitchens of the cadet mess in Washington Hall.

The superintendent's house on West Point. It sits overlooking The Plain where formal parades and ceremonies are conducted. It has been the residence of West Point superintendents since 1819.

Washington Hall where the dining hall, known as The Cadet Mess, is located. The original cadet dining hall was built on the location of Grant Hall. The dining hall was moved to this location in the 1890s. It has been renovated and expanded to its present form over three different construction eras.

Molly & Mrs. Omeara at the Superintendent's House

The resident spirit at the superintendent's house is that of a young girl named Molly. Although not the oldest spirit on the Point, she is one of the oldest spirits that has a specific link to the academy. She is also one of the more pleasant spirits at the academy. No moaning or shrieking for Molly. No tale of tragic death or unfinished business binding her to the material world. Molly is quite possibly nothing more than the case of a spirit that is too lazy or simple-minded to be bothered with passing on.

In life, Molly was one of the housemaids for Sylvanus Thayer. Sylvanus Thayer was the third superintendent of the academy. Although two superintendents preceded him, Thayer is often referred to as the "father of the academy" for his single-mindedness of purpose that he brought to the position and his selfless dedication to ensuring that the academy became one of the best universities in the world.

One of the changes that Thayer brought to the academy during his tenure was a rigid adherence to discipline and an unbending respect for rules and order. It might seem odd to some then that he would have kept around a maid who had such an intermittent relationship with reliability and attention to detail. Thayer, however, modified his devotion to order with a good degree of mercy and good humor. This good nature of the superintendent was likely the reason then that Molly retained her position in the home.

Molly's employment at the superintendent's home initially was a result of well-planned and long-term nepotism on the part of her mother. Mrs. O'Meara, Molly's mother, was a recent widow living in Highland Falls in 1802 when the academy was first founded. Mrs. O'Meara was not a particularly attractive or well-connected woman and had married well out of her teens. She considered herself fortunate to get a husband at all. Her husband died shortly after Molly was born leaving with her almost no money and little hope of finding a second marriage.

Conceding that she was not likely to marry again, Mrs. O'Meara started planning at that moment to maximize her daughter's potential to marry early and to marry well. Since there were no good familial connections, Mrs. O'Meara decided that the best potential source of future husbands for her infant daughter was the newly founded university. She applied for a position as a cook at the school and was soon hired. Through hard work and diligence, she eventually became head cook at the school.

The idea was that if she worked at the university and constantly had her daughter around eligible young men, the odds were in favor of one of the young men finding her daughter appealing. Mrs. O'Meara could envision the courtship, the eventual marriage, the exciting career of the young officer as he progressed in position and authority. Usually in her envisioning, she saw herself being brought to live in the officer's some-day grand home as sort of a dowager head of household; organizing social events and balls and ensuring that her daughter and son-in-law had a properly managed staff to ensure their continued advancement.

This was not to be the case. Molly was certainly more attractive than her mother but on the spectrum of attractiveness, "more attractive than her mother" was much the longer side of the line. The best that could be said about Molly was that she was plain and was not unpleasant to look at. At an academy that was restricted to men only, this might actually have still been enough to garner some young man's attention had her personality been more appealing. Unfortunately, as with her appearance, Molly's personality was rather plain also. Certainly not in any way rude or harsh or offensive, Molly did not, however, shine.

Mrs. O'Meara did not help the matter any by not insisting that her daughter receive an education. She felt that it was much more important for her daughter to learn skills in the kitchen, and so at a rather early age, she began to bring her with her to work in the kitchen. She also was aware that her daughter was not the most attractive of young women and so felt that the exposure to the young cadets could never begin early enough. She did not find the idea that a young 17- or 18-year-old cadet might meet her 10- or 11-year-old daughter and then grow comfortable enough with her to marry her when he graduated four years later to be distasteful.

Mrs. O'Meara soon realized that this was not likely to happen in the kitchen, however. The only time Molly received any exposure to the cadets was on those few occasions when she would assist in serving at the tables. This allowed only the briefest and most cursory interactions. Mrs. O'Meara began looking around for a position where Molly would have opportunities to meet for extended periods of time with some of the young men.

The position that became available at the superintendent's house was perfect. It was a respectable position. It paid well. And most importantly, it allowed her the opportunity to meet with the cadets. Especially during the early days of the academy, there was not a single cadet that did not on an almost weekly basis have some reason to come by the superintendent's home. Molly would be there to greet them when they came to the door, take their hats and coats, ideally find something to clean in the parlor while they waited for the superintendent and engage them in conversation. Mrs. O'Meara had been working at the Point for just over thirteen years at this time and knew everyone. She even had some not inconsiderable influence when it came to matters of personnel and employment in the non-military, non-academic operations of the post. It was not difficult for her to obtain the prime post for her young daughter.

It quickly became apparent that Molly would not likely be successful in marrying a young officer, even in her position of increased accessibility. Her success as a housemaid was also highly suspect. It was not that Molly was lazy exactly, it was just that she seemed to be easily distracted. She would begin a task only to wander off and leave the task thoroughly unfinished. Even when she did finish her tasks, it was often difficult to tell. When asked to make the beds, the head housekeeper would often follow up and find sheets untucked, pillows unfluffed, and comforters wrinkled. She was never certain whether Molly had wandered off in the middle of the chore or whether Molly simply considered the shoddy disarray to be a job that was completed.

She would have been fired shortly after beginning her position had it not been for two things. The first was the housekeeper's nephew. Mrs. O'Meara ensured that the intermittently sober young nephew of the housekeeper had a position as a delivery boy and general handy-man in the cadet mess. In exchange, the housekeeper suffered the lack of reliability of Molly. Additionally, the one positive quality that Molly did possess was a sense of genuine honesty. No matter the lack of physical attractiveness or the dearth of intellectual acumen; the absence of any real work ethic or the paucity of any type of follow through, Molly was absolutely straightforward. There was no obfuscation on her part. If she did not complete a task and was asked about it, she would simply tell you. If she was dressed down about dust on a mantle or the state of a parlor rug, she would very frankly tell you that she really didn't see the need to do any better than what she had done. In an environment that was often over-flowing with people needing to be thought better of than they actually were, it was refreshing to be around someone who simply didn't care. Although this lack of concern of other's opinions sometimes came across almost as spoiled, most people appreciated this refreshing bit of careless innocence and so Molly continued in her position for several years.

As the years passed, Molly progressed through those ages that all young girls of that time inevitably faced; blushingly hopeful young girl, carefree placid young woman, and then ultimately progressing towards the more matronly adjectives. The chances of her becoming a beautiful young bride became more and more distant but it did not change Molly's attitude or her actions. She maintained her blissfully uncaring outlook.

Molly's mother, Mrs. O'Meara was not so untouched by time. She had proceeded her daughter through these stages by almost a quarter of a century. As it became more and more apparent that Molly was never going to become the bride of a promising young officer and less and less likely that she would wind up becoming anyone's bride, Mrs. O'Meara became more and more bitter. The realization that she would never be the respected head of an officer's home but would in fact likely never become anything more than the head cook of the cadet mess, forced to cook and wait upon others, twisted her mind and her outlook. She became increasingly angry and abusive to all of those around her. She would suffer from tyrannical outbursts of shouting and was even known to throw utensils and pans if angry enough.

Disease Strikes

The end would come for Molly first. As New York became a larger and larger city, hygiene became an issue, and with it, disease. Disease was always a concern for any large city and New York City was no different. Influenza, tuberculosis, small pox, and cholera, among others, would strike the city from time to time and sweep through the confined, filthy spaces like a raging fire. After the War of 1812 had been concluded, New York City grew at an even more rapid rate. It swelled rapidly with immigrants and was visited by sailors, merchants, and visitors from all around the globe. These visitors brought with them not only the latest stories and fashions, but also the latest diseases and epidemics from every port in the known world.

During one of these outbreaks of some unknown disease that was only vaguely defined as "the great flu," thousands of New Yorkers became ill and hundreds died. Those that could afford to, left the city in droves. One of these wealthy citizens that fled the city was a friend of the superintendent's and was invited to stay with him at the superintendent's home on West Point. Unfortunately, however, he did not flee soon enough. He became ill with "the fever" and suffered for the better part of a week and a half in the superintendent's guest room. The post doctor came and ministered to him and gave strict instructions to the staff as to how to handle any of the bedclothes or garments that were soiled by the guest.

Molly's poor work ethic literally became the death of her. Whether it was mishandled sheets or perhaps failing to wash her hands properly or maybe simply forgetting to wear a mask when in the vicinity, the results were the same. As the guest recovered, Molly became ill. Soon it was Molly herself that was laid up in the bed in the guest room being tended to by the physician. It was no use. Of less than average intelligence, looks, and perseverance, her constitution proved to be no different. She soon faded and in less than six days from the moment that she first fell ill, Molly died right there in the room.

Mrs. O'Meara had spent much of that week tending to her daughter. Those who did not know better thought it touching that the older woman was so obviously desperately trying to help her daughter recover. Those who were among the household staff and witnessed the whole thing, however, knew a different story. Mrs. O'Meara berated the sick girl as if it were something that she had done intentionally to spite the older woman. She acted as if Molly had gotten ill for no reason other than to rob Mrs. O'Meara of her last hope that she might someday be part of a successful and respected household. After Molly's death, Mrs. O'Meara became inconsolable for a very brief period and then, much to the chagrin of those who worked there, returned to the kitchen with even more anger and bile than she had previously visited upon those unfortunate enough to work with her.

Quickly after Molly's death, strange events began to be reported around the superintendent's home. A bed would be freshly made and then only moments later would be found to have corners untucked and blankets ruffled. Rugs that had just been taken out and beaten would be almost immediately infused with dust. An entire sink full of freshly washed dishes would be discovered to be covered in food. Trimmed lamp wicks, that had only moments before been burning cleanly, would suddenly be found inexplicably too long and smoking terribly. At first, the head housekeeper thought that everyone was simply using the excuse of Molly's death to slack off in their efforts. She soon realized that this was not the case when items that she had inspected or personally cleaned herself were suddenly filthy and disorderly as soon as she left the room.

It was not difficult to link the death of the young maid, Molly, to the rash of strange incidents. Although there certainly might have been a maid or two who used the ghost of the departed girl as an excuse, it clearly seemed more than a case of mass laziness. The reports were too numerous and too consistent to dismiss. It was almost as if the young woman were still employed there since. All of those tasks that she had failed to accomplish successfully while alive never seemed to be well accomplished after her death. Additionally, the playful spirit seemed not content to simply reenact her poorly done chores. Soon she was adding to her repertoire of tricks by moving objects about the room and even mischievously hiding things from guests and staff alike. The superintendent at one time even asked Mrs. O'Meara to come back to the house and "talk" to her daughter but the now older and increasingly bitter Mrs. O'Meara refused. Eventually, everyone got used to Molly's post-mortality antics as they had become accustomed to her pre-morbidity actions. Her spirit settled in as simply another member of the household, albeit an unseen one.

The older, living Mrs. O'Meara was not so easily tolerated. She was still shy of fifty years old when Molly died but it seemed to transform her instantly into an old woman. She became more bitter as each day drew her further and further away from the dream she had once had of a life of leisure. As that dream became fainter, she made sure that the reality for everyone who worked for her was anything but leisurely. She worked long, hard hours and insisted that everyone around her do the same. The hard work seemed to give her strength. Instead of growing weaker as she aged and pushed her body to the limits, it seemed she found strength in her close-souled bitterness.

Almost as if to spite those around her, she lived for an incredibly long time. It was not until 1857, when Mrs. O'Meara was north of 80 years old, that it finally looked like she was going to find any rest. One day, when she failed to show up for work, a maid was sent to her rented flat in Highland Falls. The maid found Mrs. O'Meara lying cold and stiff on the floor of her bedroom. The staff and faculty at West Point held a funeral for her, but it was more out of a social necessity than it was any real affection for the old woman. It was interesting to note that even though she had served for over forty years of her life at West Point, there were not the number of mourners at her service as there were at her daughter's.

It was not until after the death of Mrs. O'Meara that any truly unsettling events began to occur at the superintendent's house. Many people believe that spirits remain behind when there are injustices or unfinished business in life, or perhaps when the body and spirit are separated in a particularly sudden and violent manner. In Mrs. O'Meara's case, the unfinished business was very obviously the marital state of her daughter, Molly. Although Molly was dead and had been for quite some time, it did not seem that Mrs. O'Meara's spirit was quite ready to give up on her once-grand fantasy. (No one is quite certain why Molly's spirit remained behind. It is not likely that she stayed behind to finish her chores, since she seemed to care little for them even while alive. Most folks who are familiar with the case believe that it is most likely that Molly was simply too lazy or flighty to bother crossing over.)

Many people have reported that laughter in the house, especially the laughter of a young girl, has been known to be followed by a stern, disapproving voice. Mirrors in the house on many occasions have been known to reflect two overlapping images of rather plain and unattractive women; one a woman in her mid-twenties, and the second, a gnarled old woman of 80 or older. Those who were unfamiliar with the story have assumed that it was some sort of moralistic warning along the lines of the *Portrait of Dorian Gray* but those who knew the women in question said that the images were those of the elder and younger O'Mearas. The undone chores that were the mischievous work of the spirit of Molly took on rather creepy overtones when they were visibly seen to be corrected. A made bed would suddenly appear wrinkled, then, before the startled spectators' very eyes, the wrinkle would once again be smoothed out as if an unseen hand were straightening the sheets and ensuring that the house were perfect. It was the spirit of the older O'Meara correcting the mischievous actions of her daughter.

More with the O'Mearas

In addition to the hauntings of the superintendent's house, the cadet mess also began to be haunted by Mrs. O'Meara's spirit. Pots and pans would fly off of their hooks and hurtle through the air at servers who were too slow or at cook's assistants who dropped a utensil or botched a recipe, just as they had been hurled by the hand of Mrs. O'Meara when she had been alive. Serving maids would feel their hair being pulled roughly or their faces would sting at the slap of an unseen assailant. Oddly enough, there was never a report of an incident involving Mrs. O'Meara at both the cadet mess and the superintendent's house at the same time. It was as if the spirit of the elderly O'Meara was still constrained by the physical restrictions of having to travel the distance from one to the other.

Kitchen staff and superintendents over the next fifteen decades would report these incidents. Most of them bore the good-natured mischief of Molly and the slightly sterner intervention of Mrs. O'Meara with a sense of humor and a grain of salt. Others simply refused to acknowledge anything out of the ordinary was happening no matter how often it occurred or how directly it impacted them.

One of the more famous incidents occurred when the commandant of the Coast Guard Academy was visiting the superintendent of West Point and was a guest in his home. The room that had been carefully made up for the Coast Guard commandant was found to be in an embarrassing state of disarray when he arrived. The bed was not only wrinkled and ruffled but the blanket was actually half off of the bed and the pillows were strewn around the floor. An apologetic superintendent had the room set to rights quickly and the commandant and his wife had their luggage unpacked and their clothes and personal items stowed neatly away.

Upon returning from dinner, the room was once again in a mess. The commandant's wife's personal things had almost all been taken out and scattered about the room. The superintendent was now embarrassed that one of his staff had apparently gone through a guest's things and had not even been subtle in doing so. The staff was immediately called on the carpet but no culprit was found and the blame was quickly laid at the feet of Molly. The superintendent was familiar with Molly and her antics but had never known her to act so outlandishly. He was not certain whether to accept the supernatural explanation or not.

There were one or two more incidents that evening but the final straw came the following evening. The commandant's wallet disappeared out of his jacket pocket. The jacket had been hanging up on the back of his chair while he had been sitting in the chair, working on a speech that he was to deliver in a few days. It was unknown how anyone could have gotten the wallet out of the jacket while he sat practically on top of it.

The wallet was not found that evening despite a thorough search. The following morning the wallet was rediscovered but in a most unusual and unsettling way. When the commandant and his wife awoke the next morning, they found that during the night someone had packed the commandant's wife's valise and had placed it on the bed between the two of them while they slept. Under the valise, beneath the sheets of the bed and lying between the commandant and his wife was the missing wallet. No reason and no explanation could be found for the incident. It was no wonder that the two guests left the superintendent's house that morning and checked into the Thayer Hotel. (This did not guarantee that they would not be further disturbed by ghosts since the Thayer Hotel has plenty of spirits of its own but as far as can be determined they did not suffer from any additional incidents.)

This incident reportedly occurred during the early seventies, a time of rather marked activity by many of the supernatural guests of the Point. A few years later, the wife of LTG Goodpaster apparently was bothered by another string of rather memorable events at the house. The end result of these incidents was that a few female cadets were allowed to stay in the homes overnight and record anything unusual that occurred. This seemed more a good-natured nod to the mostly friendly spirit of Molly, however, and was not so much a serious inquiry into the nature of the haunting.

Additionally, we are including a memo from Lieutenant General Knowlton, and a series of correspondences between him and the official post archivist and a renowned psychic who was called in regarding the "sense" of the place and the mysterious disappearance of a certain bed that was of historical significance.

MASP   25 October 1972

MEMORANDUM FOR: LIBRARIAN

SUBJECT: Quarters 100

1. As you know, last week there was a lecture by Mr. and Mrs. Warren who have had extensive experience with the spirit world and the supernatural. As a result of this, the lady came to Quarters 100 in view of the reports of spirits still living in the quarters. The paragraphs below give you the results and also ask some questions.

2. In the second bedroom back on the south of the second floor, young Sam Koster reported awakening one night and finding a lady in the room in a long white dress. When he challenged her and asked who she was, she went out through the door. Mrs. Warren walked into that room and immediately said, "There is a lady in this room. She is not old, very domineering, athletically inclined, and really not quite a lady. I get a feeling of no man; if she had a husband he was dominated while at home." After her lecture she came back and had a short seance in the room during which she opened the window of the unoccupied house (we were in New York) and attempted to gain contact with the spirits. What she had on her hands was one irate spirit who took umbrage at the earlier discussion and did not wish to be bothered or contacted. She did get, as she went into detail, a jumble of impressions of many other people - but many families have lived in that house. Question: Is there a Superintendent's wife or sister who would fit that description in past history?

3. The room across the hall is the room in which the Superintendent of the Coast Guard Academy and his lady found in the early morning hours that someone had removed Mrs. Thompson's wallet from her handbag and placed it carefully between the two of them. Mrs. Warren says that spirits do move things in that fashion, not maliciously, but to gain attention. In that room, however, Mrs. Warren received no vibrations or feeling of anyone - male or female.

MASP   25 October 1972
Subject: Quarters 100

4. The front room on the south carried an impression of happiness and of young
children. The VIP bedroom which used to be the master bedroom carried the
distinct spirit impression of an older couple who were very much a team, liked
to collect things, and were greatly interested in the quarters. The quarters, of
course, contain the collection of furniture, silver, etc. belonging to General and
Mrs. Conner who fit that description and who probably lived in that room.

5. In the basement offices of Sylvanus Thayer, Mrs. Warren immediately encountered the spirit of a man who was very decided, had no particular interest in
women, and who did not like to entertain except when business required it.
Question: Sylvanus Thayer? The minute she entered the orderly's room, without
knowing the purpose of the room which could easily have been Colonel Thayer's
bedroom, she encountered a totally different spirit -- young and mischievous.
That is the room where the bed is occasionally messed up and where legend says
the orderly has returned and messed it up to gain attention. One of the things
which startled us is that she felt very strongly in that area the presence of a
Black American named Greer -- tall and slender, in a gray uniform with no
collar. I note that the picture of the quarters in my office taken in the late 1800's
shows the Superintendent and his lady seated on the front porch, and a Black
orderly standing at the entrance to the downstairs offices in the right background
of the picture. Question: Do we know if the quarters ever had an orderly named
Greer assigned who was a Black American?

6. They also encountered a young woman named Beulah, but have the feeling that
she was a niece of someone stationed there rather than a servant. Question: Is
there any documentation on her?

7. In her battle of wits with the strong willed woman in the second floor bedroom,
Mrs. Warren received the distinct impression of a large and old canopy bed in that
room. I am told that somewhere the Post Quartermaster has an old canopy bed
which came out of the Superintendent's Quarters 20 or 30 years ago. Question:
Do we know what room that old canopy bed was in?

8. I find myself fascinated with this particular escapade, and cannot help but
wonder whether some of it is borne out by historical research.

                        WILLIAM A. KNOWLTON
                        Lieutenant General, USA
                        Superintendent

                                2

Pers in file for rec. AR 340-15; the permanent copy is to The Adjutant General's Office.

Superintendent's Memorandum of 25 October 1972 Concerning Quarters 100

TO Librarian, USMA	FROM Chief, USMA Archives	DATE 3 Nov 72	CAT 1
		Mr. Tozeski/rmh/2017	

1. Since the USMA Archives is a repository of official records only, there was little chance of finding answers to the Superintendent's questions up here. However, we have spent considerable time searching through what we do have hoping for a few leads. Some of the things mentioned are based on tradition and myth and would, of course, be difficult to track down. It would require an extensive search of reminiscences etc. which are not part of the Archives holdings.

2. Reference paragraph 2, Supt's Memo. Generally speaking, there is very little information on the family (wives, children, household members, etc.) of the Superintendents. Descriptions of any sort are lacking. Such a woman -- "not old, domineering, athletically inclined, and not quite a lady" might describe anyone from Sylvanus Thayer's Irish cook "Molly" to General Benedict's sister-in-law! The former is often cited as the "female ghost of the Thayer rooms" who kneads bread in the kitchen and rumples up the bed coverings.

3. Reference paragraph 5. Sylvanus Thayer remained a bachelor but some descriptions of him state that he was most gracious with females and an excellent host who entertained visitors and staff members regularly. As evidenced from his accomplishments during his tenure as Superintendent, however, Thayer was definitely a "very decided" person.

4. Reference paragraph 5, latter part. We had a little more to go on here, i.e. a specific name. There have been several cadets with the name of Greer from the Civil War to the present, and even a couple of instructors. None of these, as far as I could determine, was black. There have also been three enlisted men with that name, and for a time that looked promising.

    a. A Private James Greer was a member of the USMA Detachment of Cavalry during the 1870's. Men from that detachment were detailed to extra duty as saddlers, blacksmiths, hospital nurses, and orderlies to the Superintendent. Such details were not always done on written orders but appeared on monthly detachment returns. We have only scattered returns for the cavalry detachment from 1867-1874 and none of these show Greer detailed as orderly to the Superintendent. A check of correspondence of both the Adjutant and the Superintendent failed to turn up anything. Unfortunately we do not have letter books of the detachment.

    Private Greer transferred to the Engineer Detachment in 1883 and was retired as corporal in 1897. There was no entry in the orders or correspondence book indexes for him during that period. His service record in the National Archives is not likely to show internal assignments, but would probably disclose his race -- something we cannot determine from records here.

DA 2496   REPLACES DD FORMS, EXISTING SUPPLIES OF WHICH WILL BE ISSUED AND USED UNTIL 1 FEB 63 UNLESS SOONER EXHAUSTED.

MALI-A   3 November 1972
SUBJECT: Superintendent's Memorandum of 25 October 1972 Concerning Quarters 100

   b. A *Private Frederic C. Greer* of the 29th Ordnance Company transferred to
Rock Island Arsenal in March 1926, according to USMA Post Orders. We have no further
information on him.

   c. *General Prisoner Lawrence Greer* was definitely black, formerly a private
in Troop C. 9th Cavalry. He escaped from confinement at Fort Leavenworth in June
of 1931 and was apprehended the following April near Albany, New York. He was
brought to West Point and court-martialled for his escape and subsequent desertion.
Found guilty, he was sentenced to 2 1/2 years hard labor. However, the sentence
was disapproved by command of BG Connor because the prisoner was judged insane at
the time of his trial. We have no record of what happened to this Private Greer
after these events.

   d. The picture referred to by the Superintendent is in our files and titled
"Superintendent's Quarters ca 1870-1. General Pitcher and Wife." The individual
near the entrance to the downstairs offices does indeed appear to be black. This
was probably a butler or other servant personally hired by the Superintendent and
not an enlisted man officially assigned as orderly. (According to the Cavalry
Detachment returns for 1871 the man then on that detail was a Daniel Cavanagh.)
Regrettably, there is simply no way of tracking down such servants other than in
personal correspondence and reminiscences of the Superintendents. These are not
in the Archives, and little if any are in Special Collections.

5. "Beulah" drew a complete blank. Virtually no leads, other than Thayer's
reportedly having a niece who stayed with him for a time (per Katie McGuinn.)

6. Mr. Gene D'Onofrio, Family Housing Division, informed Ken that during his time
of employment (over 20 years) no canopy bed from Superintendent's quarters was over
turned in to his warehouse. He indicated they have a bed that is said to have been
in the possession of President Fillmore. He also stated that Mr. Rostanza made up
two beds that are presently in Superintendent's quarters. He believed canopies
could be used on these if desired. He hasn't the vaguest idea of the whereabouts
of the canopy bed in the Superintendent's Memo.

                              STANLEY P. TOZESKI
                              Chief, USMA Archives

2

After almost 200 years of residency, there are now more than just these two ghosts that reside in the superintendent's abode and make their presence known from time to time. The story of Molly and her mother are, however, still the most well known and most frequently observed. Their tale is still told and retold with each passing superintendent and each change of resident. Even today, most superintendents are more than willing to pass a moment or two with you, discussing their own personal incidents. But if you are ever fortunate enough to be invited over to this historic residence as a guest for the evening, or even overnight, make sure that you put your valuables away and that you keep a close eye on your keys and wallet or you might find yourself in a fruitless search while the ghost of a mischievous young girl laughs at your discomfort from a century away and right over your shoulder.

2130 - arrived; received tour of useful facilities
ie refrigerators and bathrooms and light switches
We smoothed the bed and stretched a wool blanket
to see if any indentations are made. Very
lumpy bed, may be hard to tell
Turned the bread board over - wet on both sides
Spread tissue on it to see if anyone sits on it.

[icon] partition Turned off some of the lights (kitchen area)
We've also been invited to a breakfast of waffles at 8:00am

2200 - Flashlight check reveals nothing new
Reggie & Rita are doing engineering. I am doing ART

2222 - I put out some coke & a cookie for the ghosts

2230 - No discrepancies

2253 - A lot of pacing - Rita gives a "boot removal" demonstration

2300 - Reggie is still doing engineering - with the intent of
putting himself to sleep. Rita is _____
I am playing solitaire. It is cooling off down here - esp in the office
No discrepancies

2330 - No discrepancies

2400 - The witching hour is here. Now, where are the spooks?
It is much cooler than when we first arrived

0030 - Reg. is taking her sleeping shift. Rita & I were talking about the
"Amityville horror" house. The cookie is still intact, no coke gone, no spirits

0100 - Still nothing. Rita & I are playing concentration. Reg is keeping the floor warm.

0130 - Very very cold in the office. We're all at watch now. Nothing is happening

0200 - Nothing again - Studying & card playing help the time to pass quickly. We're now being more careful about noise discipline

0230 We turned the ouija board right side up again and replaced the tissues. Maybe we horrupsed the spirits too much. Reg is studying. Rita & I are pacing. Nothing has happened thus far and we're over 1/2 way done

0300 Still nothing. Rita sat for a while in the library and we were all generally very quiet. Maybe the ghost took a weekend. Reggie is still trying to study. I'm just distracting everyone.

0330 This last hour was marked by no unusual activities from the psych side of the house. Of course, we have now taken our souvenir pictures — Rita — staring dull-eyed into space, and Reggie "dead" at the table — engineering finally got to her. This is a far cry from the eagle-eyed ghost hunters who arrived 6 hrs earlier! However, we will persevere until the job is done (or 0600 - whichever comes first). Rita wants me to mention myself. Fortunately, I don't have to. That's the historian's prerogative.

0400 Rita & I are playing cards in the office. We can hear Reg rummaging for food in the other room. Otherwise — silent! I take that back — we found a spider.

These documents reflect a letter to LTG Goodpaster. The tongue-in-cheek recording of the female cadets' overnight stay at the superintendent's house and their interactions with Molly. Interestingly, the letter that the female cadets actually penned to Mrs. Goodpaster is curiously missing from the West Point archives.

0430 No Discrepancies

0500 Same - Card playing (800 mill games of crazy 8's, concentration). Reg is now keeping the table warm.

0515 Rita & I try to build a card house. She gets the giggles → earthquake.

0530 We began to clean up - Not that we made a mess, you could just tell we'd been here - Thayer never drank coke and Girl Scouts weren't invented until later.

The West Point train station as it looks today. This is not the structure that stood on this spot when the train station was first opened and the events that left such a dark mark upon the cadet's pleasant evening occurred. The original structure was damaged in a fire and then was later torn down and replaced completely.

This is a photo taken looking back up the river, the now corrected bend where the train and all of its passengers hurtled into the dark depths of the Hudson River.

3
The Fall Social

The sight of a train chugging through the idyllic setting of the Hudson Highlands is a common sight to those living on West Point. The sound of the whistle echoing up the hillside is a reassuring sound to many. But to those who have heard the whistle when no train is present or have seen a train as ethereal and opaque as the steam which rises from its smokestack, the sight and sound can be terrifying. For those who have gotten close enough to see the faces of the doomed passengers through the cloudy window or hear their screams as they hurtle to their demise, the sight and sound can be life altering.

There are two different stories that are often offered as explanations for the sightings of ghostly trains at West Point. One of the incidents involves the tunnel that passes beneath the plain of West Point. The other story, however, predates that one by several years and this is the story that we will tell here.

Our story takes place in 1863, just after the rail line from New York to West Point had been completed and at a time when our country had just entered its most bloody war ever. The train station that now sits at the landing at West Point would not be built for another sixty years. In its place was a larger but simpler structure. This was the terminus for passenger travel from New York City on the western side of the river. There were only two reasons why this western line even existed. The first reason was the battle between rail tycoons that was going on, spurred by Pullman's contract disputes, political aspirations, and overall over-inflated egos. The line on the east side of the river belonged to a rival rail baron and the western line was built in an attempt to put the eastern line out of business. The race for dominance and the corners that were cut would have dire consequences in a very short period of time.

The second reason that the line was built was West Point itself. Although you could reach Albany on the line on the east side of the river, there was no direct line to West Point. If you wanted to come to West Point, you had to disembark at the Garrison station on the eastern side and then take a ferry ride across the river. Even worse, many suffered the rough fifty-mile ride up from the city in carriage or on horseback. For the soldiers and the cadets that frequented West Point, this mode of travel was certainly not out of the question, but West Point was quickly becoming a social destination for the ladies in the area and these accommodations were not always suitable.

Only 60 years old at the time, West Point was already one of the leading engineering universities in the world and a repository for some of the finest and brightest young men from socially connected families in the United States. Columbia University and Yale were the only comparable concentrations of eligible future husbands in the New York area and neither of those had the added appeal that the flair of an Army officer had to offer. Ladies' colleges and finishing schools in New York and Connecticut would arrange trips to West Point for dances and other social events. Some would say that it was the mothers of future brides who had as much to do with the rail line to West Point being constructed than the rail barons themselves.

One of the biggest social events at West Point every year was the fall dinner and dance. It was held every year at the end of October. Young ladies would come from all around the area, trailing chaperones and luggage behind them, and quickly fill up the hotels and inns anywhere within five miles of the post. Homes were opened up to guests and the entire area would take on a festive nature for those few days. The weather at that time of the year, however, would make the trip miserable for some and impossible for others.

It was with much fanfare then that the line to West Point was completed and the station was finally opened. From the moment the line opened, people were looking ahead to the West Point Fall Dance. The weather would not be able to keep anyone away. Those who previously might not have been able to come because there was no place to stay, now had the option of making the entire journey, there and back, in a day. This was certainly going to be the biggest and most extravagant dance the Academy had ever seen and was destined to be one of the high points of the New York social season.

Thus was the stage set, October 31st, 1963. It had not been planned as a Halloween dance but the Saturday of the dance just happened to fall on Halloween that year. No one viewed this as an ill omen. If anything, the holiday simply added to the festive nature of the event. A band had been engaged to play on the train to make sure that everyone was in fine spirits when they arrived. A very fortunate group of five young men, cadets from the Academy, had been selected to come down and greet the young women as they arrived and serve as their escorts on the ride up the Hudson River.

Groups of young women from three of Manhattan's finest schools were gathered in Penn Station that afternoon as well as a group from the Finchley School from Connecticut. In addition to the school groups, many daughters of prominent state and national figures waited along the benches, anxiously discussing how best to get a young man's attention with their mothers or chaperones. Among the prominent young women in the station were Emmeline Bathhurst, daughter of the president of the stock exchange, Susan Fisher, daughter of the Fisher Carriage Company founder, Evelyn Fisher, Susan's mother and a millionaire in her own right as the heiress to one of the largest sugar plantations in Haiti, the niece of the governor of New York, the governor's sister, a senator's daughter, and many, many more.

All of these anxious people were totally unaware of the tragedy that was about to occur. As is the case with most tragedies, it was only through a series of events that this misfortune was able to take place. Most are too momentous to simply occur on their own. In this case, the first of the series of events had certainly nothing of the sinister about it, although it did involve death. A mule had died crossing the Brooklyn Bridge. This was certainly not something that would have normally impacted the anxious young women at the station or the even more anxious young men at West Point who were awaiting the anxious young women. In this instance, however, the mule happened to be part of a mule team that was pulling a cargo wagon across the bridge. When the mule died, it spooked the other five members of the mule team and they all bolted. The end result was that the wagon overturned and the roadway across the bridge became clogged with boxes and bags and tangled traces. The two carriages that were bringing young ladies from the day school in Brooklyn just happened to be caught in the jam that piled up behind the wrecked wagon. They were an hour late in arriving at the station. The conductor only momentarily entertained the idea of leaving without them but he knew that there was a little bit of time built into the trip for delays. It also was likely not lost on him that the daughter of the railroad owner happened to be on one of those carriages.

After the late arrivals took their places and bags were stowed, all was ready to go. They would have just enough time to make it to the Academy by this point. It was at this inopportune moment that the collier for the train discovered that the coal that had been loaded into the coal car was of an inferior grade. The sulfur content was much too high and there was a great potential for damaging the boiler if the pressure got too high. The conductor and the collier, after much debate, decided that they did not want to risk the boiler blowing out on them on the trip and so more time was lost as the coal car was disconnected and a new coal car was attached behind the engine. This required much coupling and uncoupling of cars which wound up delaying them another forty five minutes.

The five young cadets did not seem fazed by the loss of time. This delay simply meant that the time they had with these young women, exclusive of the rest of the corps of cadets, would be extended. For all they cared, the wheels could fall off the train and they could have the ball right there in the station. The young ladies were thankful that they had at least these five young men to speak to, but they had not put on their best dresses simply to be looked at by only five young men, regardless of how dashing or respectable they might be. They wanted to get to the dinner and the dance. Still they made the best of it. At the behest of the chaperones, the band struck up a reel and dancing commenced on board the train while it was still changing coal cars.

The train finally began to build up steam and prepared to leave the station. The girls and their chaperones knew that they had now missed most of the pre-dinner social hour and were concerned that they might miss the dinner itself. This meant that their window of time for pre-screening and filling their dance cards was rapidly diminishing. Through a combination of cajoling, threats, and outright bribery, and under the glares of a half a dozen anxious mothers, the conductor promised to get them to West Point in time for the dinner. (The rumor was that Emmeline Bathhurst's mother had offered the conductor the equivalent of two months pay if he could get them to the Academy "rapidly." There was an implied addendum that there might be no forthcoming salary ever again if they were less than "rapid.")

The threats and bribes were barely necessary for the trainmen, however. Train men are of that breed that prize punctuality and speed above all else. At that time, fastest speeds between important stations were often posted in the stations. The conductor and the brakeman relished the opportunity to open up the engines and try for a new, New York City to West Point record. The train fairly flew up the river. The engineer and the brakeman worked in perfect synchronization. Instead of slow, careful decelerations and accelerations around curves and over hills, the two men focused on sudden and aggressive changes to the speed of the locomotive that barely kept the train clinging to its track. They were making excellent time and were on a pace to easily beat the previous record as they passed the station at Tomkin's Cove. The men were already thinking of how they were going to spend the bonuses that the mothers had offered to pay them.

The final turn before the approach to the West Point station is not the same today as it was in 1863. The turn back then was a wider turn. In their haste to finish the line, the decision had been made to build the final turn out on piers over the water instead of taking the time to blast a part of the cliff to make the run a bit straighter. The engineer blew the whistle as they approached the turn to let the station at West Point know that they were arriving. The young women on the train broke out in cheers. All along the stone wall overlooking the station, the young male cadets echoed the cheer. They had all come out to welcome the young ladies as they arrived and had been waiting anxiously this last hour. Anxieties began to drift away as everyone turned their thoughts to the pleasant dance ahead.

The anxieties of the brakeman and the engineer began to increase, however, as they entered that final turn. The brakeman threw the lever to decrease their speed around the turn but nothing happened. The rapid and aggressive braking that they had done on the trip up from the city had finally taken its toll on the brakes and the gear snapped. The brakeman attempted to engage the emergency brake but the heat and the friction had fused the coupling open. The brakeman immediately signaled the engineer to cut the power to the engine but it was too late. Frantically, the brakeman began racing up the railcars from the back, shouting to them to get down on the floor and away from the windows. Laughter and gaiety turned to panic and confusion in his wake. The reality of the danger was just beginning to set in as the front of the train entered that final, fateful curve. Many continued to dance, oblivious to the impending disaster. An unlucky few fully grasped the gravity of the situation, if not the specifics, and began screaming in horror. The speed of the train, mercifully, did not let the screams continue very long.

The heavy engine almost made the turn. The engineer felt the car began to lean. For a moment it seemed as though the wheels reengaged the track and it appeared that all might be well but then the lean continued. The left side wheels began to pull at nothing but air. The tipping point was reached and the engine hurtled off the track and into the depths of the Hudson River, a mere hundred yards away from the station and solid land. Like obedient children, the coal car, the passenger cars, and the brake car followed the engine, urged on by centrifugal force and their own momentum.

The spectacle was witnessed by all of those waiting at the station and watching from vantage points along the stone wall above and even from the roofs of convenient buildings. Family, friends, and the entire corps of cadets watched in horror as the river ate the train cars one after the other. An unholy silence gripped the valley as the last car disappeared beneath the water and the imperturbable Hudson River flowed on above the carnage.

Immediately, the West Point cadets and faculty sprang into action. Some rushed to the nearby boat dock and began to untie the boats. Others rushed to the newly completed station and began grabbing up or tearing off anything that would float. Others simply leapt into the dark waters without a thought as to their own personal safety. Cadet Sellers was one such rescuer. He leapt into the dark waters but was not seen again.

With a rapidity that only military engineers could muster, there was soon a floating bridge of sorts above the site. It was made up of two row boats, bits and pieces of loose lumber, mooring lines, a bench, and, still recognizable amidst the mayhem, a large section of the station ticket counter. Cadets and faculty, with ropes tied around their waists, were diving into the waters trying to locate the train cars or any survivors. Lanterns were brought to illuminate the dark scene. For every light that arrived, a dozen twins were born on the ripples of the river that flowed past. The bell from the station continued to toll as it had since the tragedy first struck, adding a mournful soundtrack to the macabre scene.

The fall dance would not occur this evening. The search continued. All through the evening more boats and more lights arrived. They held out hope that one or more of the rail cars might have a pocket of air inside that would keep some of the girls alive. This hope would, unfortunately, not come to fruition. As the night rolled into the following day and the first stray rays of the sun began to struggle upwards, the most eerie moment of the entire accident occurred. The usually turbulent waters of the Hudson cleared for just a moment. The rays of the sun that should have been streaking upwards from a sun that was still below the horizon, suddenly angled downwards, filtering through the water. Rescue workers on the boats and the makeshift bridge above the site looked down into the suddenly still and illuminated water and gasped. What they saw in the water forty feet below them were the errant strands of light weaving their way through the cold, green water, and through the snaking rays of light; dancers. Beautiful young girls with smiles on their faces, their hair floating around their shoulders, were moving in rhythm as though gravity were not an issue. Holding their hands and moving with them were the young cadets in uniform who had accompanied them on the train, as well as Cadet Sellers, who had disappeared under the water in the first moments after the crash.

As quickly as the vision had appeared, the silt and vegetation shifted in the stream, the light returned to its normal place in the sky, and the vision vanished. All of the rescuers who labored on the boats and rafts and who had seen the sight, quietly put down their tools and made their way back to shore. Those still on shore and those who had not seen the dancers in the waves continued working and called out to ask why others were leaving. What was there left to say? They knew that their efforts were futile.

The official search was called off several hours later. Unofficially, many family and friends continued searching for days; if not for survivors, at least for a body or something which they could lay to rest in memory of their lost loved ones. No body was ever found.

Investigation a Tragedy

An investigation was launched into the cause of the accident. It was determined that the speed of the train, the condition of the brakes, and the curve of the track had all contributed to the crash. The decision was made to blast part of the bluff away and change the angle of the final approach to the station. This was done, the new track was laid, and the station was reopened ten months later.

The following year, the dance that never occurred was scheduled again. Many had called for the Fall Dance to simply be cancelled permanently, but others felt that holding the dance would be the best way to put the tragedy behind them. An excited but more subdued group of young women left Penn Station on time. An excited but somber group of young men awaited them at the Academy. They arrived with no complications. The social hour progressed and then it was time for the dinner. Everyone was finally starting to relax and allow the spectre of the previous year to fade away.

Then, just as they were sitting down to eat, from down the river came the frantic blowing of a train whistle. The guests all startled. The train that they had taken sat at rest in the station waiting to take them home at the end of the evening. There was no other train scheduled to arrive at West Point until the following day. Many at the dinner who were aware that this was about the time last year that the wreck had occurred got a queasy feeling in the pit of their stomachs. Most people shook it off and returned to their dinner but several excused themselves from the table and went outside to the stone wall overlooking the river.

The accounts they gave were chilling. They came from more than a dozen people, so it was hard to dismiss them all as hallucinations or fanciful tales. What the witnesses said that they saw was a train coming down the track, shimmering like the ever present Hudson Valley mist. Music could clearly be heard coming from the train although it was impossibly far away. Visible through the lighted train car windows were the images of young ladies, dancing hand in hand with cadets in uniform.

The misty train hurtled down the final stretch toward the station but inexplicably curved out over the water where there was no track. Then, in a frightening replay of the previous year's events, the engine tipped over into the water and then the entire train spilled into the river. The witnesses also claimed that as the train descended into the depths, not a single ripple formed on the surface of the water and not a hint of a splash was heard. Perhaps the most frightening image of all that was reported, was that even as the train turned on its side and entered the water, the dancers visible through the windows never faltered in their steps and the smiles never faded from their faces.

This is one of the few tales that occurs with predictable regularity at West Point. The train has been seen by cadets, faculty, and guests at West Point around the same time every year. Most people in the area can hear the whistle but simply believe that it is a normal train on a normal track making a normal run. Others have actually been able to see it from the bluff or the road above and have seen the terrible crash replay itself again and again every year. A few adventurous souls venture down to the dock on these evenings and have been given firsthand accounts of seeing the floating, dancing, drowned young men and women, not realizing that they have already met their end. Not a Halloween night or a Fall Dance has gone by since that evening that the fall dance train has not been spotted. It is always there; still racing to try and make it to the dance on time and still destined to forever fail.

4
Benedict Arnold and the Ghost of Major Andre

The next tale that we will tell takes us back to the time of the American Revolution. It involves a man whose name has become synonymous with the word "traitor." There are many stories involving Benedict Arnold and West Point. More than one or two are of the ghostly variety. Since Benedict Arnold actually escaped to England after his treachery and died a lonely man, eking out a meager merchant's living, it is unlikely that his ghost ever returned here. If someone begins regaling you with stories of ghostly sightings of the traitorous general at West Point, tell them they need to re-read their history books. You should have no concerns about hearing their stories after midnight. Their ghosts are nothing but sheets on a string.

There is, however, at least one very dramatic ghost story relating to Arnold and his attempt to turn the fort at West Point over to the British.

For those of you who may not know, in 1777, General Arnold was the instrumental planner in the strategic victory at the prominent battle of Saratoga. It was a key early victory for the Americans. Many thought that his success would lead to him replacing Washington as head of the Army. At the very least, it was certain that a promotion was in line.

Neither of these things happened. Perhaps Washington was jealous of Arnold's success. Perhaps Arnold's arrogance and unconventional tactics had made him more enemies than friends. Perhaps it had something to do with charges that Arnold had misappropriated funds or that he had "lost" a payroll chest with $50,000 in gold coins. Regardless of the reason, Arnold became convinced that unless the colonists changed tactic, they were bound to lose. Arnold did not plan on being on the losing side.

The hillside where Major Andre hid his cursed treasure hoard—treasure that was already stained with blood and which would have been used to further a traitor's goals had he succeeded.

One of the many rocky outcrops and overhangs that
Major Andre could have used to store his hoard.

British spies were aware of this breach between Arnold and Washington and sought to exploit it. Arnold was approached by the spies who played to his arrogance and his greed. He eventually agreed, at least conceptually, to become a traitor to the cause of the revolution. All that remained was for the details to be worked out. Initially, Arnold had demanded 10,000 pounds, a pension, and compensation for his losses during the war. He raised his demands several times, eventually topping out at 20,000 pounds, but then lowered the demands back to his original offer of 10,000. Because of the inconsistent nature of the messages going back and forth, the offers and counter-offers were not always in synch. As a result, Arnold never knew that the British command had actually agreed to his demand for 20,000 pounds and the British did not know that he had reduced his fee to the 10,000-pound original amount.

On the morning of 21 September, 1780, Major John Andre, the adjutant general of the British forces located in New York City and chief of spies for the British commander, boarded a sloop and sailed north up the Hudson River. The name of the sloop was the H.M.S. *Vulture*, an appropriate name for a vessel engaged in such a felonious act. As the day was drawing to a close, rowers put Major Andre ashore at a point just below the town of Stony Point. From there, Major Andre began the overland portion of his journey to meet up with Arnold. This was where things would get a bit hairy for the major. Not only was he traveling through enemy territory at this point, but he was doing so in civilian clothes. He was a spy. A soldier in uniform would be captured and imprisoned, but there was always the chance that they might be exchanged for American prisoners. A captive soldier also knew that at the end of the war he would go home. Spies had no such assurance. If spies were caught, they were hung.

If that threat were not bad enough, Major Andre was also carrying a satchel with 10,000 pounds in coins and jewels, a down payment for the surrender of West Point. In the flux of authority that existed during this time of conflict, there were many bandits in the area that owed allegiance to neither side and would gladly have killed for much less than 10,000 pounds. Major Andre had been instrumental in getting General Clinton, the British commander, to agree to the increased demand of Arnold for 20,000 pounds, and had likewise convinced Arnold to accept only 10,000 pounds. Since only Major Andre had access to all of the letters that were exchanged between Arnold and the British, he was the only one who knew all of the offers and counter-offers. It was his intention to only pay Arnold the 10,000 that was being held in an account in New York City. He planned to keep the money and jewels that he carried in the satchel for himself.

He thought that this could be easily done and covered up since the money and jewels had not come from the British treasury in the first place.

Earlier in the year, the British had sent a force up the Hudson River and had been successful in taking the town of Tompkins Point. General Clinton had intended to use the town as a base of operations from which to attack West Point. It was much closer than New York City and it would have been easier to supply an army besieging the fort from Tompkins Point than it would have been from the city that was fifty miles away. The locals who were loyal to the American cause and the ever-present militia that harassed the lines between Tompkins Point and New York City soon made this position untenable. General Clinton was forced to withdraw, but not before going on a rampage of despoiling and pillaging. He confiscated everything, food, livestock, and money, in the name of the king. (Much of the wealth, however, actually never made it into the king's coffers and more likely found their way into Clinton's pockets.) One particularly wealthy Dutch family, the VanNuygens, refused to surrender their wealth or swear allegiance to the crown. General Clinton, or perhaps one of his officers, had the family murdered and their property seized. Their wealth consisted of enough coins and jewelry to line General Clinton's pockets and also supply the additional 10,000 pounds that Major Andre insisted Arnold needed.

The blood wealth of the murdered VanNuygens was what now weighed down Major Andre's satchel. He planned to find a convenient and identifiable spot to stash the loot and then return for it after the fighting in that area was over. As he made his way to his rendezvous with Arnold, his path led him dangerously close to the fortifications at West Point. This was tricky but necessary since he needed it to be close by a settled area. He could not risk losing the satchel in the middle of the woods somewhere. He found what he considered the perfect spot. A small cave near the mouth of a spring provided a spot that could be easily relocated but out of the sight of any casual observers. It was large enough for a grown man to lie down and squeeze into. Extended at full arms length, the satchel was placed on a small niche at the back of the crawlspace.

Having satisfied himself that his fortune was made, Major Andre continued on to his meeting with Arnold. Arnold confirmed that he would accept the offer of 10,000 pounds being held on account for him. He had also brought the plans for the fortifications at West Point with him, as well as the location of the troop distributions. Major Andre was ecstatic. Not only had his mission been a success but he would soon be 10,000 pounds richer in the bargain.

Major Andre took the plans from Arnold and began to make his way back to his rendezvous point with the H.M.S. *Vulture*. This rendezvous, however, would never take place. Major Andre had wasted too much time searching for a hiding place for his loot prior to meeting with Arnold. As a result, the H.M.S. *Vulture* had been spotted and fired upon. The sloop had been forced to withdraw. Major Andre was now faced with the daunting task of traveling the entire distance back to New York City and friendly territory on foot.

He actually was close to accomplishing his goal when he stumbled upon a sleepy militia outpost on the Tarrytown Road on the morning of Saturday, September 23rd. The militia outpost was primarily concerned with troop movements coming out of New York City and was not prepared for a single individual moving the other direction. Major Andre was almost able to talk his way out of their hands but something about his mannerisms, or perhaps his appearance after having already walked almost thirty miles, hinted that something wasn't right. The militia men searched him and found his papers from Arnold. After he was identified as a spy, no amount of talking could free him. He offered them huge amounts of money but the militia men were loyal to the cause and refused to release him.

Andre was brought before a military court the following day. On October 2, hardly more than a week after his capture, Major Andre was hung.

A Treasure Lost

Major Andre would never retrieve his treasure during his lifetime but there are many who say that he will not be parted from it in death. The first account of Major Andre's ghost haunting the area came the very evening of his execution. A two-man sentry patrolling the area around West Point reported seeing a man in the woods. When he would not respond to their demands to identify himself, Private David Milliken fired a round from his rifle at the figure. Though having been placed on sentry duty for his exceptional marksman skills and considered by many to be one of the best shots in his unit, Milliken appeared to miss at a distance of what he judged to be no less than fifty yards.

From the sentry's log, evening of 2 October, 1780:

CPL Taylor reports that on sentry with P Milliken, vicinity of Dale's Woods above, two shots fired at unidentified intruder, no action follows.

This incident was further clarified in an excerpt from Milliken's journal that was published in the *Mills Ledger* later that winter.

CPL Taylor and I sighted a man moving through the woodline near the upper road. CPL Taylor demanded a halt, which the gentleman did not seem inclined to obey. Hastening along the road to the point in the verge, I saw ahead of me a distance of fifty yards, a man in traveling dress. Calling again a command to halt which, being not obeyed, I drew and fired. Certain of my shot but no lag in the step of the gentleman being shown, [Taylor and I] drew [pistols] and followed up the slope. It seemed to us odd at the time, or at least upon later recollection, that there was no sound from the man being pursued but only the brush that Taylor and I trampled. Of a sudden, we came upon the man stooped to the ground. First thinking he had fallen to my shot, but then showing no ill signs or responding to entreaties, it did seem, but unlikely, that he had stooped to drink at a small spring flowing from the rocks. I stepped to within a pace of the man, at which point he sprang about to face us.

I have not seen such a face outside of first light on a yesterday's battlefield. The skin...I cannot say but to say that it hung like loose cloth dampened by a mist. A horrid black ring encircled the neck, rising to the chin from whence the face was as white as a page of paper but for the eyes which were red and full of blood. It, and I say it at this point for it seemed so little like a man, shrieked like a protesting mill wheel. I fired straight into its breast with the pistol. It would be impossible for me to miss at this point but it showed no sign of stopping as it rushed at me and passed me, seeming almost through me and leaving me chilled through the coat and to the skin. Being startled for only a moment, I turned to pursue but saw no one. Taylor and I searched the area for several minutes but found no one nor any sign that either of my shots hit true.

CPL Taylor did not keep a log but confirmed the story in an interview with the Ledger.

There were several more unconfirmed reports during the durations of the war. It became a running joke with soldiers assigned sentry duty in the area. After the war ended, there were no more sightings of Major Andre for many years. The story died away and was mostly forgotten. Then thirty-five years later, the War of 1812 broke out and sightings began again. By this time, West Point was serving as the United States Military Academy. Many cadets who had no knowledge of the previous sightings, reported seeing the apparition. Their stories were eerily similar. A cadet who was walking through the woods around the base for relaxation or perhaps returning from a tryst with a girl from the local area would encounter a man dressed in traveling clothes that were quite outdated. The appearance of the man was invariably described as ghastly white, with skin like damp cloth, and a horrible black bruise encircling the neck. He was usually seen in the vicinity of a small spring in the area.

The story was not known in its entirety until after the War of 1812 was over. As part of the treaty that ended the war, many personal papers of captured soldiers on both sides were returned to their families or to their government. Many of these papers went as far back as documents that were captured or kept from the American Revolution. At this time, the amounts of money offered to Benedict Arnold were well documented, as well as the duplicity of Major John Andre who attempted to enrich himself through these actions. Even two of the militiamen who originally captured Major Andre, Isaac VanWaart and David Williams, mentioned the incidents in their diaries. After the extent of the treachery was exposed and connections were made between the apparition and Major John Andre, reports of the apparition increased, although most were simply written off as popular hysteria.

The next confirmed report was not until 1864. A senator whose son was attending West Point was taking his horse out for a ride when he spotted a ghastly figure in clothes that were almost a century old at that time. The figure did not respond to his calls so the cadet followed him. He almost caught up with the figure at the edge of the wood line but then lost time as he had to dismount and follow on foot. The cadet came upon the creature stooping near a spring in the rocks just as Milliken had reported. And just as Milliken had said almost ninety years earlier, the figure turned and, as the senator's son reported, "seemed to pass through me, chilling me as though it were made of ice."

He related the story at dinner that evening to his father, who was in town visiting, and to General George W. Cullum, the superintendent of the academy at the time. The superintendent, who was familiar with the story, reportedly told the senator that he had seen the ghost of Andre himself while serving as a cadet at West Point. (There are no reports of this outside of this conversation so it is entirely possible that General Cullum was engaging in a bit of colorful remembrance.) Major Andre's ghost may be one of the few ghosts in American history that actually has been recognized, in a manner of speaking, by the United States Congress. The senator, whose son had reported the sighting and who had heard the story of Major Andre from General Cullum, made a comment during a speech that a Union victory was "as certain as it is that Major Andre will continue to return to his ill-fated treasure at West Point."

Major Andre has continued to appear intermittently over the years since then. He seems to appear most frequently during times when the U. S. is involved in a conflict, as though the unrest gives added strength to his restless spirit. The most recent credible sighting happened in 2004 when a plebe (a first-year cadet) got separated from his team during the Patton Challenge, an event that takes small teams all around the base. The plebe spotted an oddly dressed figure moving through the trees and thought it was an upper-classman attempting to add a historic element to the challenge. He approached the figure and called out "Cadet Chrispyn asks a question, sir." Once again, the only response was a shriek from the figure as it turned and rushed the terrified plebe.

The plebe reported the incident when he returned and it initially got entered into the Central Guard Room log. An honor violation was actually initiated because it was thought that the plebe was making up the story to try and explain why he had gotten lost. Upper-class cadets, however, who were familiar with Major Andre's story quickly intervened and the matter was dropped.

There has been an increase in sightings again during the recent conflicts in the Middle East. Treasure hunters and ghost hunters alike have come to the area in search of treasure or answers or both. The area that Major Andre's ghost is suspected of frequenting most often, lies somewhere on the hills behind the old cavalry barracks. This area now lies between the base bowling alley and the new housing development on top of Stony Lonesome. Those who have encountered the ghost themselves describe it as the most terrifying experience of their lives. They would recommend against seeking it intentionally. But, if you do ever happen to encounter this pale, strangled figure bending over in the woods near a mountain spring, mark the place well. With a little bit of patience and minimal digging, you might wind up with a treasure that is valued at around $750,000 today and might even help a spirit find rest in the bargain.

5

The Haunting of Henry Hudson

The story of Major Andre and his ghost is an old one at West Point but it is certainly not the oldest. The oldest written account goes back almost 200 years previous and involves the area of West Point adjacent to the river and almost immediately behind the Lee Housing Area. Henry Hudson, the "discoverer" of New York Harbor and the Hudson River, wrote about an incident that happened to him and the crew of his ship, Half Moon, here in 1609. Hudson was the first European to set eyes on the Hudson River Valley and the piece of land that would eventually become the United States Military Academy at West Point. Perhaps "ghost story" is not the best description of the events, but there is often not a clear definition for many things that fall outside the natural realm.

On September 11th, 1609, Henry Hudson began sailing up the river that he initially called the North River, but would later be called the Hudson River. He states in his ship's log that he arrived at the port that would later become Albany, New York, ten days later. The date that was written in the log, however, was September 22nd. That is a difference of eleven, not ten, days. This is the story of that missing eleventh day.

It is impossible to tell where exactly Henry Hudson would have put to shore. The very nature of the story makes the geography itself suspect. This is, however, one of the many streams that flows in the general area and is close by the Lee Housing Area where many of the sightings of the strange man and his ethereal guests have occurred.

This story may explain why Hudson continued to return to North America over and over again over the next two years, even though he was often strictly forbidden not to by his employers. It might explain why Hudson's men mutinied on one such trip in 1611 and cast him adrift, claiming that he was "a man possessed, not of a sound mind". It might explain why those mutineers, although obviously guilty of Hudson's murder, were all set free upon their return to England without serving a single day in prison. It might also explain the most puzzling part of the Hudson mutiny mystery; why it was that witnesses claim that they saw Hudson cradling a young boy as his ship drifted away, even though no boy was listed as a sailor on that voyage.

A Voyage

On September 11th, Henry Hudson and his crew entered the upper harbor of New York. Guiseppe Verrazano had discovered the entrance to the harbor eighty years previously but no one had ever sailed into the interior to see what it held. Hudson hoped that it might hide the secret to the elusive Northwest Passage. What it held was certainly a secret but not the one that Hudson was hoping to find.

The voyage began rather mundanely. The first two days passed with no incidents. Hudson spent most of his time exploring the area of the bay and by the 13th was anchored off an area near present-day Yonkers. The following day, however, the river journey began in earnest. By the morning of the 16th, the ship had already progressed past Bear Mountain. A water cask was opened that morning but the water inside was found to be quite foul. The water inside had been contaminated by some filmy algae. There was water enough to last them in other casks so Hudson directed that the foul water be dumped over the side so as not be used mistakenly. The mundane incident became a near tragedy, however, when a sailor who was wearing a golden ring got his finger caught between the edge of the barrel and the railing. The sailor might have lost his finger had not the blood from the deep tear caused the ring to finally slide off his finger and into the river. He was of course upset that he had lost a valuable item. To hear him swear and wail about the loss of the gold one would have thought he would rather have lost the finger.

Almost immediately after the incident, the ship rounded a bend in the river and was presented with one of the most perfect little river bays that a captain could wish for to dock his boat. The land, which in the highlands area is normally steep and rocky, sloped gently down to the river. On both sides, the cliffs menaced the river but in that one spot it was grassy and smooth and free of rocks or trees. Additionally, there was a clear stream rushing down the side of the meadow and into the river. Hudson had originally decided that since they were far from desperate for supplies or water, they would not stop to refill the foul cask for several more days. This seemed like too good an opportunity to pass up, however, so the decision was made to anchor there for the night, refill the water cask, forage for any additional food that they might be able to find, and then depart the next morning.

The ship anchored and Hudson went ashore in the longboat with seven individuals. The boat pilot, whose name was recorded as J. Haskins, two rowers named Wuerthal and Brioard, three unidentified sailors, and a young man named Jan, no last name given.

Author Note

This last individual has created issues for many historians. Accounts of the mutiny of Hudson's crew on the ship *Discovery* two years later state that a boy named John, and identified as Hudson's son, was one of the individuals who was marooned with Hudson and six other crew members. There are no accounts, however, of a teenage passenger named John ever being on the manifest of the *Discovery*. Some historians believe that the young boy named Jan that was listed on the 1609 voyage was actually Hudson's son and claim that the dates and time of his demise are confused. Others believe that Jan was actually an illegitimate son of Hudson and John was a totally different person. You can read the story, do the research, and then decide for yourself.

Upon stepping ashore, the first order of business was to clean and fill the tainted cask and store it back on the longboat. The party rolled the barrel across the gentle landscape to the stream. As they got closer to the stream, an outcropping that had, from the ship, originally appeared to be a deadfall of trees, began to look more and more like a man-made structure. It was along the stream but further uphill from where they were filling the barrel. It was intriguing enough that they left the barrel where it was and climbed up the hill to investigate. What they discovered upon arrival was that it appeared to be an oddly constructed sluice box. Hudson wrote in his log that "it must have been most curiously constructed for it seemed to sluice of its own accord by some mechanism of the stream else some invisible man did manipulate it so."

Almost as surprising to them as the mechanism of the sluice box itself, was simply the fact that there was a sluice box there at all. This meant that there were people there; people who were civilized enough to build a complex device. Since Hudson thought that he was traveling through undiscovered territory, this came as quite a shock to everyone. Additionally, the presence of a sluice indicated that someone at least suspected that there was something worth sluicing for in this wilderness.

Upon looking into the sluice box, the object of the unidentified builder became quickly apparent. There were several easily visible nuggets of gold lying along the rails of the box. They were not insubstantial in size. A conversation quickly broke out among the party. Peripherally was the issue of who might be out in what was considered unexplored territory. What country might they be from? What were their claims in this new land? Central to the discussion though was what to do about the gold. The purpose of the voyage was one of discovery, but discovery for commercial purposes. The people who had hired Hudson thought they could make money off of his efforts. Why waste time and effort struggling to find a passage to Asia if gold was plentiful in this new land was the gist of the conversation that was breaking out among the party.

A Strange Man

In the middle of their discussion, a man stepped out of the woods across the stream and walked up to them. Hudson would reflect later that in hindsight the man would have had to have crossed the stream to get to them but no one could recall seeing him enter the water or being wet upon arrival. There were so many other strange things assailing them at the time that this one additional oddity did not strike them until later. The man's appearance certainly did strike them, however. It had been supposed by the group that if there were indeed a man out there in the wilderness, he would likely be a striking pioneer of a man, dressed in the roughest of garments and probably living hardly better than an animal. This was not the impression that they got when the man approached.

He was short, likely not more than four and a half feet tall, and very round. Not just fat, but actually round. His shoulders sloped out and downward. His thin chest never dipped back in to denote the presence of a waist but continued in a curve that terminated at a pair of thin and unusually tiny feet and ankles. A bushy beard filled in whatever gap existed between the face and the shoulders so that the overall effect was of a great ball. The man's face was bright, ruddy, and very smooth. The eyes, nose, mouth, and ears seemed as unusually small as the feet.

The man wore a hat. No hair appeared straying from under the edge of the hat. The hat itself was as odd as the rest of the individual. The brim was so broad that, had the short man not been looking up, it would have completely obscured his face. The crown of the hat sloped back to a two-inch circle in the center from which rose a stove pipe-looking peak. It was easily another two feet in height and flat on top and terminated just above the heads of Hudson's party.

The man's shirt was a long-sleeved verdant green top that appeared to be velvet. This luxurious looking top was tucked into a pair of brown, buckskin breeches that were tapered and were themselves tucked into the tops of black boots with curiously pointed toes. Topping off the eclectic outfit was a flamboyant maroon cloak that was clasped with a thin, intricate gold brooch.

The party's reaction was of course one of great surprise, not only at his appearance but at the fact that there was a European, albeit an odd-looking one, so far away from any known settlements. Hudson immediately addressed the man and asked him who he was. The response, as Hudson reported, was perhaps even stranger than his appearance. Hudson wrote that the strange man repeated back exactly what Hudson had said, using the same inflection, and in a voice that was unsettlingly familiar to Hudson's own. Hudson repeated his greeting and the same repetition occurred again. Hudson began to become annoyed, thinking that he was being mocked, but then he thought that perhaps the man spoke a different language. The sailor, Brioard, who was with them thought that perhaps the man might be Dutch and addressed him in Dutch. The same scenario repeated itself. The man repeated exactly what Brioard had said, using Brioard's same inflections and accents, and sounding very much like Brioard himself. Another of the sailors spoke a bit of Portuguese and attempted to speak to the stranger but the results were the same. Hudson also commented in his journal that he noticed at this point that the man was not only repeating them when they addressed him but he was also repeating bits and pieces of their conversation as they discussed how best to communicate with this enigmatic stranger.

Hudson began attempting to communicate with the man using signals; pointing to the boat in the bay, the barrel by the shore, the stream, and of course, the gold. At this point, the man suddenly began speaking to them. This struck the group as odd since he had seemed unable to do anything but repeat words previously. What struck the group as even more unusual, however, was the manner in which he communicated. Although he was no longer repeating verbatim what the group members said, his words continued to be exact duplicates in tone, volume, accent, and inflection to the words that the crew used. It was like listening to sentences that were strung together with words spoken by the crew themselves.

Another oddity regarding the man's appearance and demeanor was the way that he would stretch up onto his toes and then settle back down on his heels as he talked. The constant rocking back and forth gave the impression that the man's height was actually changing. At least one of the shore members commented that it seemed less like he was leaning up and settling back and more like he was flowing up and down. As if his body, or at least his skin, was some type of liquid.

Hudson would record that it was determined that the man must be either Belgian or possibly Swedish, due to his rapid comprehension of the language. It seemed remarkable also that no matter how much comprehension that he exhibited, they never seemed able to understand exactly where he came from. He seemed confused when they asked and simply told him that he was from "here," which they assumed meant that he thought that they were asking him where he lived. He was cordial enough though and invited them on a tour of the area. He showed them the sluice box and attempted to explain to them how it worked. He showed them a path in the woods which they declined to explore at that time and then right inside the edge of the woods he showed them his hut. He was even hospitable enough to ask them if they would like to spend the evening with them in his hut.

Hudson was hesitant to accept the man's invitation since the hut that they were directed to did not appear to be more than ten feet square and wasn't likely to be able to hold more than two or three people at best. Not wanting to seem rude though, he said that they would go to the hut. He planned to use the excuse that he needed to return to his ship to politely leave at a later time. As with the man though, the hut turned out to be more than its appearance initially indicated.

The difference between the inside and the outside of the hut was so enormous that initially, Hudson said, his impression was that they must have stepped down as they entered the hut so that they were below ground, or perhaps the hut had been built into the hill. The interior that was spread out before them was vast and warm. There was a large living area with an expansive hearth and at least two doors and a hallway leading out of the main room.

The oddities began to quickly multiply as dinner was prepared. A sense of unease began to permeate Hudson's shore party. Fires were started under the pots and pans without any apparent use of a flint and steel or tinder of any kind. Pots and pans seemed to get filled without anyone remembering the odd little man actually putting anything in them. The man was observed setting the table but it appeared that for every plate he put out, at least two or three place settings were left in his wake. The group agreed, in hurried whispers, that they would not eat any of the food or drink offered to them until their host had eaten them first to make sure that they were not poisoned.

They did not have to wait long. Their host started in immediately without any formalities. After only a brief glance around the table at each other and a moment's hesitation, they all joined in. The dishes were as varied and delicious as they were endless. At the time, no one seemed to notice, or care, that the serving plates never seemed to empty. And it never occurred to them until later either that a tray that had been full of venison one minute, was filled with pheasant the next.

At the end of dinner, the host offered his guests tobacco for their pipes. And somehow without any effort from the host, the table was cleared as they filled their pipes and lit them. As they relaxed and smoked their pipes, the host rose from his chair and went over to a small chest and withdrew a cloth bag. He carried the bag to the center of the room and opened it. Had they not all been so full of good food and so relaxed from the warm fire and the tobacco, they would have cried out in astonishment. The bag was full of gold nuggets.

The host then made an unusual offer. He said that not only would he help them clean out and refill their cask but that in addition, he would give them the bag of gold if they would leave one individual behind when they sailed away. The group considered the proposition. Certainly none of them were willing to volunteer to stay but they felt fairly certain that if one of the sailors on board the ship saw the accommodations that were available here they would be more than happy to trade their berth on the ship for the land-bound luxury. Additionally, they figured that leaving a person behind, a colonist so to speak, they would have even greater legal authority to claim this rich land upon their return. The lure of the gold could not be dismissed either.

In the end they agreed to accept the offer. The host handed the bag over to Hudson. He then startled them by pointing at Jan, and demanding that the boy be the one that was left behind.

Hudson of course immediately objected and rejected the offer. He tried to return the gold but the host insisted that they had a bargain and that Hudson now had to live up to his end. Hudson became angry and went to draw his sword, as did one of his men, but the sword never left the sheath. Publicly Hudson would later claim that he did not draw his sword because he had wanted to settle things civilly with discussion first. Privately, however, he would admit that he tried with all of his might to draw his sword but it would not leave the sheath.

The host seemed distressed by the angry outburst and immediately attempted to calm the situation down. He apologized and blamed his unsocial behavior on his lack of contact with other people for so long. He told them that if they would be his guests for the evening and entertain him with stories and conversation, he would send them on their way in the morning well-rested and with the chest of gold regardless.

The group accepted the invitation. In discussions afterwards every individual man said that he wanted to leave but that he didn't want to speak up because he thought everyone else wanted to stay. They did all agree, however, that at least two men would remain on watch at all times. This resolution did not last much longer than it took their host to escort them down the hall and into a sleeping chamber. The room, oddly enough, had exactly eight beds in it; one for each member of the party. As soon as they entered the room, an overwhelming lethargy struck them and they fell into their beds with almost no resistance or hesitation.

The following morning is best experienced through the actual words of Hudson's log.

The morning broke hard upon us and rather late. By the position of the sun, it was near nine of the clock. The position of the sun, late as it was, was less troublesome than the image of the sun itself. The room in which we had laid down had no windows through which to view such a sight. The room was gone, as were the beds upon which we had slept and, in point of fact, the entire cottage itself. Had that been all that was amiss, it would have been our assumption that we had been transported in our wine sodden sleep to awaken upon the hard, damp ground. Beyond the mere hut being gone however, the entire gentle slope, the grassy field, and the gentle stream were missing. We were reclined upon a stony, wooded cliff above a rocky shoreline, a distance off which was anchored our ship. A quick search was made but no sign of our host, his dwelling, or our initial welcome landing site could be found. It was but a moment until we heard a shout from the ship and a signaling shot fired. Quite alarmed we became when we heard an answering shot from a distance of but three hundred yards to our side. Thinking that but for ourselves and our now missing host we were the only inhabitants of this land, it startled us to think that yet another unknown person or persons was in the near vicinity.

We were very relieved then when moments later, we heard shouts in good English following the shot. We quickly shouted a response and had a moment to assess our situation as they made their way toward us. All were silent, staring about with wonder as the impossibility of our situation repeatedly beat in upon us. It was as if there were a collective fear gripping us all that froze the air in our throats until at last the silence was broken by brave little Jan. With a single tear running down his face, he began repeating, "What is it Captain? What is it?"

Barely keeping the terror from his voice, he kept repeating the same phrase over and over again. I, for all of my experience and all of my love, had not even the courage of the boy to break the silence.

It was at this point that the sounding party found the confused men. The story that the first mate relayed to them did nothing to explain the event and in fact only deepened the mystery. The first mate said that they had waited on the ship for the captain's return. When night fell they became concerned and determined that at first light they would send ashore an armed party to ensure the captain's safety.

Early in the hours of the second watch, however, a cataclysm occurred that no one as yet could understand. The watch sounded the alarm, which was immediately followed by the violent sound of water crashing on stone and the even more ominous sound and shudder of wood on stone. All hands poured onto the deck and were stunned to see in the moonlight, a towering rocky cliff jutting out of the shore line where a safe cove had once been. The first mate began shouting out commands to move the ship away from the threatening rocks while simultaneously cursing the watchman for allowing the moorings to slip and letting the ship drift into this precarious position. The watchman began babbling, saying that he had not allowed the ship to drift and claiming that before his eyes the cove itself had suddenly disappeared and become an unfriendly anchorage. The first mate, initially not believing him, locked him up in the brig for drunkenness on duty and intended to give him a lashing as soon as it was day.

The ship was then moved into the center of the channel and anchored once again. The first mate did not want to try navigating back to the safe cove that they had previously been anchored in with only moonlight to guide him. An unknown river was no place to be maneuvering at night and so they waited, with increased watch, for morning.

At first light, a sight more frightening than a loose mooring or a drunken watchman awaited them. The cove was gone. Their natural instinct of course was to disbelieve what they were seeing, but it was hard to deny the fact that it had simply disappeared. The bend in the river and the island opposite it were distinctive. It was next to an impossibility that two stretches of river could be that identical. There could be no mistake. And yet there had to be, for there was no cove. The assumption was that if they had drifted during the night, it would have been downstream but this was not an area that they had previously passed. This had to be where they had anchored. They spent the entire morning sailing back down the river to the point where the two sides of the cliff rose up steeply on both sides of the river. It was exactly as it should be. They sailed back upstream and there was their anchor point of the previous day but the pleasant shore line was simply missing.

A Curse?

It was not until late in the day that they accepted the impossible and words like "enchanted" or "cursed" started being used. Many of the men were all in favor of setting all sails and hastening home as soon as possible. After much debate, however, it was decided that they would anchor as far from the shore as possible and wait for the next morning. In the morning they would try putting to shore and searching for any sign of their missing comrades. They went to a one-third hands watch throughout the night but few slept regardless of whether they were on shift or not.

As soon as it was light, a well-armed party had gone ashore. They had struggled to find a place to land on the rocky shore and had worked hard, once landed, to reach the edge of the rocky cliffs above. They had kept constant visual checks with the boat, never straying far inland. Apparently, someone on the boat had spotted the lost party first. They had called out to Hudson and had fired a shot to alert the search party. The search party had returned back to the edge of the rocky cliff and seen the signal from the boat and fired a shot in return.

Both parties were overjoyed that the other was safe but became even further confused when the timelines were finally compared. The first mate swore that this was the third day. They had anchored and Hudson had gone ashore on the first, the boat had sailed around trying to find themselves on the second, and then this was the third. Hudson and the shore party were just as adamant as the first mate that this was only the second day. They had come ashore yesterday, spent the night, and then had awakened this morning, the second day. No one could account for the discrepancy or the shore party's lost day. Nothing else at that point had made sense either, so it seemed pointless to debate it further.

Hudson determined that no more time should be wasted in that enchanted land and that they should depart immediately. With difficulty, they made their way back down the cliff to the rocky shore. There they found Hudson's long boat, the cask of water sitting up in the back, moored there alongside the boat the first mate and his crew had taken. Some of the sailors were hesitant to board the boat or take the cask back with them, but Hudson, much more pragmatic, did not wish to lose anything else on this ill-fated shore excursion. They all boarded and rowed for the Half Moon. All sat silently contemplating the loss of a day. Only Jan's continuous whispered question broke their meditations, "What is it Captain? What is it?"

Just before they were within a rope's throw of the ship, an even stranger silence hit the boat. The quiet questioning of the young boy, who may or may not have been Hudson's son, was gone. As mysteriously as the plates had replaced themselves and the cottage had vanished, somehow, from their very midst, Jan had vanished.

Not another word was said. The broken crew boarded the ship. The ones who had stayed on board begged Hudson and his party to tell them what had happened, but there was no reply, only a hoarse command from Hudson to make way, and then he headed to his cabin. There was a tacit acceptance that no search of the area would turn up any sign of the cove, the cottage, or of Jan.

Almost as an afterthought, Hudson pulled the small bag of gold that had been given to him by the strange man from his cloak. He could already tell by its weight that it was empty but opened it anyway and looked inside. At the bottom of the bag, glinting back up at him in the cabin's dim light, was the sailor's gold ring that had fallen over the side right before all of the madness had begun.

Hudson was shocked, not understanding what the ring meant, still numb from the strange events and the loss of Jan. In a daze, he walked to the ships hold where the refilled cask of water had been stored. No one had actually bothered to look inside it once it had been carried on board. When Hudson breached the cask and removed the lid, he found the cask to be empty, with the exception of a few strangely shaped mushrooms clinging to the damp wood on the inside of the barrel.

A thought occurred to Hudson at that moment. Not a fully formed thought, but a disturbing misty form of a thought. Again, what happened next is best described by looking at Hudson's log that he kept on the ship.

Log from 18 SEP 1609:

Nerves impossibly frayed from the previous day, or days, events, who can say but it was not without warrant that my mind was assailed with diverse, ghastly propositions. Immediately rushing to the deck I did order that no thing be cast overboard, not refuse, nor food. Naught but breath would pass the rails of the vessel and that breath be as silent as one could make it. Entreaties were made but no explanation would I give for fear of these thoughts that might presage madness, yet what if it were that the water, or the place, or something in the place did read upon us desires by those things that crossed our bows.

Log from 19 SEP 1609:

We are clear of the oppressive highlands through which we sailed and I have ordered anchors to be set. Upon the order, by myself I did stand at the rail and with much tremor cast into the waters pieces of [bread]. With anxiety I waited but saw nothing untoward. For one hour we sat at anchor, the men not knowing the why. After that hour passed and no change being seen, I did order that anchor be raised and the voyage to continue and no one to speak of the tragedies visited upon us three days previous.

Hudson, as well as others on the ship, would later express that it was their fear that something lived in that area of the river that was able to pick up thoughts from anything that touched the water. The ship was in the water and so they had found a safe place to anchor. The sailor had lost his golden ring into the water and had loudly bemoaned its loss so the thing had presented them with the prospect of gold. They had poured the foul water into the river and the thing had provided them with a source to replenish it. It had taken their baser, more visceral desires and used them to take away the true desires of their heart. Nothing in life is free.

When they finally returned to New York Harbor many days later, they suffered one more loss. Brioard, one of the sailors who had gone ashore with Hudson, took tone of the small boats and a storm sail and disappeared in the night. It was thought by some that he had also come to the conclusion that the thing that lived up the river was able to grant desires or wishes. They believed it was Brioard's intention to return to that point in the river and toss a gold ducat into the river and tempt the strange man to reappear once again. No one knows if he ever succeeded in finding the strange little man because Brioard was never seen again.

And so the rumors and the stories continue. Residents of the Lee Housing Area have often spoken of seeing a strange man in the trees wearing an odd hat, vibrant tops, and buckskin pants. Sometimes he is by himself, walking in a liquid, up and down motion that seems to be more of a flow than a bob. Sometimes he is followed by spectral figures of the souls he has ensnared. Sometimes those specters bear a striking resemblance to a 12-year-old Henry Hudson.

The belief also persists. The idea that a desire communicated to the river in that area, either an object thrown into the water or a wish written upon a stone and cast into it, will somehow be able to grant that desire to the one who threw it in. Remember, however, that if a desire so communicated is ever offered to be filled by a strange-looking man in odd clothes, the price may wind up being more than you bargained for.

6

A Question of Honor

When Sylvanus Thayer became superintendent of West Point in 1817, one of the focuses of his stewardship was integrity and honor. This focus would eventually grow into what the cadets today know as "The Honor Code." The Honor Code, simply put, says that a cadet will not lie, cheat, nor steal. This code has guided the institution for over 200 years. To uphold this code, honor boards were instituted by the cadets, under the guidance of the faculty, to investigate and judge the culpability of cadets charged with honor violations and determine their fate if they are found guilty. This system has been used effectively. Rarely has it been considered that a board found an innocent man guilty. Overall, it has helped maintain the integrity of the institution with only a few notable exceptions. One of those exceptions was the robbery scandal that hit the Point in 1896.

In 1896, a series of thefts began to be reported in the small towns around the Point and even on the Point itself. The local police investigated the matter as did the military police on the base. No one was detained and no suspects were turned up. As the thefts continued, further help was sought. Assistance was sent up from the military police in Washington, D.C. Theodore Roosevelt himself, who happened to be the Chief of Police in New York City at the time, even traveled up to West Point and assigned one of his top investigators to the case to help assist the local units.

The exterior of the 1st Division Barracks. The Honor Board Room is on the top floor just to the left of the ominous tower. It is in this room that the first apparition of the wrongly accused cadet was seen. Although this room is still primarily where the sightings continue, the apparition has been known to appear in other areas of the school.

Lieutenant Detective Archie Reynolds was an astute political operative but this did not take away from the fact that he was a brilliant detective. The forward-thinking Roosevelt had served as an apt mentor for the young detective and had helped him arrive at the leading edge of forensic investigation, at least as far as it was understood prior to the turn of the century. (This advanced method of thinking by his mentor would help him become a mentor in turn to a young James Hoover. Many of the techniques that Reynolds would develop would become instrumental in helping Hoover found the institution that would become the FBI.)

The intensity of Reynold's investigation put a halt to the robberies for a while. Reynold's knew that he was on the right track or else his poking about would not have made someone nervous enough to cease their operations. The thieves' greed or impatience, however, eventually got the better of them. The burglaries started up once again. This impatience eventually led to their downfall. Previously, Detective Reynolds had been forced to rely on evidence that was days or even weeks old. Since he had located himself at West Point, he was able to be on the scene of the crime within hours. What he discovered near the crime scene were two different sets of boot prints that were different from the boots that were normally worn at the time. After making casts of the prints in plaster and doing some research, he was able to determine that the prints were unique to the type of riding boots that were issued to the cadets at West Point.

The cadets had originally not been a focus of the investigation for two reasons. One was the honor code, but the second reason was that many of the burglaries occurred in places that were too far removed from the academy to have been reached on foot in a reasonable amount of time. Now the focus shifted. It seemed that cadets who had signed out a horse from the stable would have had ample time to ride to any of the places where the crimes had occurred. Cadets began to be questioned. Although all cadets had access to the stables, suspicion began to coalesce around a group of three juniors, and it seemed that unless someone else confessed to the crime within the next day or two, the arrest of these individuals would be inevitable.

Somehow, the unlikely occurred. Although not a confession, an anonymous letter was left at the MP station accusing a cadet named Benjamin Fishman of the crime and describing precisely where in his room two particular pieces of jewelry from the robberies was hidden. Ben was a sophomore, who had had no disciplinary issues and was an exemplary student. Everyone was, of course, quite shocked. Reynolds was immediately suspicious of the conditions under which the discovery was made. He questioned the source of the anonymous letter and why it was that none of the other jewelry was discovered in Ben's possession, just the two pieces that were mentioned in the letter. He wanted to bring Ben in immediately for questioning but the military police intervened and claimed that since the cadets were on a military base, the base laws took precedence. The prevalent regulations of the academy at the time required that an honor board be conducted and any cadet guilty of a crime would then be discharged prior to being turned over to the civilian authorities. In this way, they were able to legitimately claim that no cadet at West Point had ever been arrested.

Reynolds objected but realized it would take just as long to file any protest and get a judge to rule on the primacy of the case. Since he was assured that the honor board would convene that very evening, he chose to wait. The academy seemed divided on the matter of whether they believed Ben was guilty or not. There had always been some resentment towards him from certain biased individuals based on his Jewish heritage and a small but vocal group called for his immediate dismissal without even holding a board. There were, however, just as many staff and faculty who were adamant supporters of the well-mannered and conscientious student, so the outcome of the board was far from certain.

The honor board convened that evening on the fourth floor of Nininger Hall. It had only been twelve hours since the discovery of the stolen items. It was no surprise to anyone present that Ben pled *not guilty* to the crime. It was, however, very surprising when he announced that he knew the names of the individuals involved. He claimed that he had been approached by the guilty parties after the jewelry had been found in his room. He said that there were three individuals involved and that they had promised to make it worth his while financially if he pled guilty and took the fall for their crimes. Conversely, he said that they threatened him with "dire consequences" should he choose to proclaim his innocence.

Ben claimed that no amount of bribes or threats could force him to make a false statement. The honor code to him was not simply an external academy philosophy, it was an internal way of life that had always been part of who he was. When asked to name the conspirators, however, Ben refused. As was captured in the records of the honor board of that evening, Ben made the following reply when asked why he would not indict the guilty parties if they truly existed.

> I believe that no cadet who has spent so much time at this esteemed institution, living under the watchful eye and guiding hand of honor, can turn so far away from its embrace. Right will triumph, as it always does. I am extending to those involved this chance to live honorably and turn themselves in. If they have not done so by sundown tomorrow, we shall reconvene here and that same sense of honor will compel me to reveal their names.

The honor board became incensed at his refusal to either defend himself or to name those whom he had accused. They demanded that Ben answer their questions in full but he was stoic in his refusal and steadfast in his belief that honor would drive the three cadets to confess on their own. In the end, the honor board concluded that they had no choice but to find Cadet Benjamin Fishman guilty of violating the academy honor code. They called for Ben to be placed in cadet custody and to return to the board the following evening to hear his sentence. Under the very real likelihood that he was going to be expelled and then jailed, Ben continued to insist that the spirit of honor would see to it that he remained at the academy.

Word of Ben's claims and of his ultimatum soon spread across the campus. The real culprits were now in a quandary. They had counted on Ben confessing as their only hope of not getting caught and now it seemed that this was not going to happen. One of the thieves suggested to the other two that they do as Ben had requested and turn themselves in. He thought that surely they would be more lenient if they came forward, admitted their crimes, and returned the stolen goods.

He was quickly shouted down by the other two and a new plot was devised, more desperate and ill-conceived than the first. The holding cell for cadets charged with crimes was in the basement of the First Division barracks. It wasn't really a cell at all. It was simply a room that had been set aside for the purpose of cadets awaiting trial or transfer. A rotating guard of one cadet was seated outside the door of the room while it was occupied. Since this was not an event that happened more than once in a decade, the role of guard was not taken very seriously. It was easy for two of the cadets to stage a distraction just outside the hallway where the detention room was. The plan was for the third cadet to strike the guard from behind and knock him out. Then they would all retrieve Ben and take further action to convince him not to speak.

Murder

No one ever used the word murder.

So far the only thing that any of them was guilty of was burglary and increasing the extent of their crimes was not part of their plan. The problem was that their plan was beginning to unravel, and no one had specifically ruled out the option of murdering Ben if he did not comply. The conditions were then set for things to go terribly wrong.

Things began to go terribly wrong from the very beginning. The distraction was successful in getting the guard to leave his post and come down the hall. The problem, however, was that the cadet, Lewin, who had been tasked with knocking out the guard, was chosen more for his strength than for his critical thinking skills. The object he chose to strike the guard with was not a padded but heavy piece of wood or a sand filled sock. The object he used was a paving stone that he had picked up from the courtyard outside. The force with which he wielded the stone turned out to be fatal. The guard dropped to the ground, dead. Now they had not only burglary to cover up, but also a murder. The only way to get out of it was to frame Ben for that also and then get rid of him. It was very unlikely that they would get him to confess to murder.

When Ben saw the three come into his cell and realized that the guard was missing, he rapidly came to the conclusion that his belief in their sense of honor had been misplaced. They had no intention of turning themselves in and their presence here did not bode well for him. Before he could even put up a struggle, Lewin struck him with the stone also, rendering him unconscious.

Using a utility passage and a back-stairwell, the three conspirators transported the unconscious Ben out of the detention cell and up to the fourth floor honor board room. They grabbed the cords from the drapes and using the drapes and Ben's belt, they formed a rope which they fastened around Ben's neck. The free end was looped around the bronze plaque that hung on the wall above the table where the honor board sat and Ben was lifted off the ground to hang freely above the table. The rope was tied off. It took only a few minutes for the unconscious Cadet Fishman to become the deceased Cadet Fishman. Cadet Tolliver, the leader of the group, took a piece of paper and quickly scribbled a confession to both the burglaries and to the murder of the guard. He signed Ben's name to it and left it on the table below the suspended body. They all hoped that the "suicide" and the "confession" would close the case and they would be able to get on with their lives.

Ben's "escape" and the murder of the guard was discovered as soon as the next shift change occurred. A frantic search then ensued with the word put out that Cadet Fishman must have been guilty and that is why he had killed the guard. Warnings were issued that he might be armed and desperate. It was not long before the searchers discovered the body of Cadet Fishman, still hanging in the honor board room. An announcement was made to the student body and everyone breathed a sigh of relief, no one more so than those three guilty conspirators who had caused such turmoil in the first place. Their relief would not last long.

The honor board that had been scheduled to meet to pass out its sentence to Cadet Fishman decided to meet that night, regardless of the fact that they now had no one to sentence. It was their intention to posthumously expel Ben and close the matter officially. The members of the honor board all sat themselves around the table and solemnly began their proceedings. As the last rays of the sun began to fade from the large casement window that filled the north wall of the room, and the sun sank into that time of the day that is known as the gloaming, the door at the end of the room swung open and a figure strode up to the table. The board members were at first annoyed at being interrupted and then were confused. Facing them across the table, in full dress regalia, was Cadet Ben Fishman.

"I told you that I was honor bound to return to you and to tell you the identity of the guilty party, and even death cannot inhibit honor," the spectre of Fishman proclaimed. For the next five minutes, the ghost stood there and addressed them, outlining exactly what had transpired and naming the three men involved. The stunned board could do nothing but record his statement. When he was done speaking, the image of Cadet Fishman seemed to simply fade away.

The honor board did not know how to proceed. There was no precedent for how to handle the testimony of a ghost. In the end, they found Detective Reynolds and relayed to him everything that had occurred. The apparition obviously perplexed a man who was used to dealing with facts, but he did not dismiss it. These were the three individuals who he had previously begun to suspect and this strange occurrence only strengthened his resolve to get to the bottom of the matter.

Detective Reynolds obtained a sample of the three suspects classroom assignments and compared the handwriting to that of the suicide note. He then compared these samples to the anonymous letter that had been received by the MPs. The suicide note matched the writing on Tolliver's paper and the anonymous letter matched the writing of a cadet name Secort. These two were brought in, along with Cadet Lewin. It did not take long for them after they were separated, to turn on each other and begin to implicate each other in the burglaries and the murders. Reynolds wanted to take them immediately to jail but the members of the honor board felt as if they owed it to Fishman to close out this incident according to the academy's policy and under the auspices of the board that felt somewhat complicit in his death.

With the full agreement and understanding of Detective Reynolds, the three cadets were brought shackled before the honor board. The first order of the board was to posthumously reinstate Cadet Ben Fishman and officially clear his name of all charges. The second order of business was the three thieves and murderers before them. The three men were quickly tried, convicted, and summarily expelled.

As the verdict was announced, the three men standing before the table began to shout in terror and stare at the wall above the table. The honor board, Detective Reynolds, who had been allowed to view the proceedings under these unique circumstances, and the two guards, turned and followed their gaze. All present saw the ghastly image of Cadet Fishman still hanging from his makeshift noose over the bronze plaque on the wall above the table. Even more startling was when his arm raised and pointed at the three former cadets and his rictus-ridden mouth opened. A stentorian voice proclaimed:

Golden bricks lay six by six, and silver bulls a coffer full, by the pass before the mass, now you will lay before the day."

The voice faded away and the arm lowered. Almost immediately the three prisoners were seized by a sudden inability to breath. Everyone present in the room could only watch in horror as the three fell down upon the floor and slowly but painfully gave up their lives. Any attempts to resuscitate them were in vain. As the rest of the people in the room finally gave up on the three now-dead men, they looked back up to where the image of Fishman had been only moments before, but the image had disappeared.

There was much debate as to the meaning of what the ghost had said. The threat that the three thieves would die before another day had passed was obvious and was very apparent in its truthfulness. The comments about the gold bricks and the silver bulls was less clear. It was suspected that this had something to do with the jewelry and coins that had been stolen. Many speculated that the ghost had attempted to reveal the location of the hidden cache that had still not been found so that it could be returned to its rightful owners. Some reported that the figure had said "golden bricks," possibly implying that the gold had been melted down into more easily transferable gold bricks. Others claimed that what the figure had said was "gold *in* bricks" implying that the stash was hidden behind some bricked up wall somewhere on the campus. The "silver bulls" could likewise refer to melted down silver bullion or it could mean something totally different. Others thought that it was simply a riddle that referred back to the crimes that were committed themselves and had nothing to do with any potential treasure. And some believed that this was not a description of the loot but directions on how to find it. Based on the reports of the stolen items, if recovered today, the total value of the cache might be over $100,000. Many searches have been made over the years but none of the treasure has ever been reported as recovered.

A Spirit of Honor

More significant to many people than the stories of the treasure, however, are the stories of the continued reappearance of the spirit of Cadet Benjamin Fishman. Within a year after the incident, reports started being heard that the image of Cadet Fishman would often reappear in the honor board room, particularly during those cases that were extremely difficult to adjudicate. It is said that Fishman's strong sense of honor has led him to act as an overseeing spirit of honor to help guide the board when they are uncertain. If the accused is innocent, Fishman will appear at their side, standing shoulder to shoulder with them in front of the board. If the accused is guilty, Fishman will appear above the board, still hanging from his noose, passing judgment down from on high. Most famously, the hanging image of Cadet Fishman was seen by as many as fifty cadets during the infamous engineering exam cheating scandal of 1976.

Less reliably, Cadet Fishman has even been reported to appear outside the confines of the honor hall. Cadets accused unjustly of something that might not warrant an honor board hearing will sometimes report feeling the presence of an unseen arm around their shoulder, reassuring and encouraging them. Some cadets unjustly made to do undergo physical punishment such as doing push-ups have reported that at times it felt like some unseen hands were helping them back up off the ground each time they pushed up.

And on at least one occasion, a cadet confessed to an honor violation that had not even been discovered. Although officially it was reported that it was his guilt that caused him to confess, unofficially he claimed that it was the constant image of a man, hanging from a noose, that appeared everywhere in front of him and eventually drove him to confess his misdeeds.

7
Not In Our Stars, Dear Brutus

There is a ghost that haunts the Catholic Chapel on post that is unique in its origin. Its mortal life did not end at the chapel nor was it interred in a service at the chapel. It did not attend mass and was in fact, not even a Catholic. She was a lapsed Methodist at best. Her spiritual remains are tied to the chapel only by a twist of fate and a bit of government red tape.

There is often seen a tragic figure floating about the Catholic rectory garden or through the lower level porticoes below the balcony or even on the balcony itself. She is often seen wearing a flowing white gown of the period that was common around the turn of the century. Her hair is described as being dark and having an auburn tinge. Her face is not pale as many ghosts are described, but is instead bright and pink, with a slightly darker complexion. Other than the outdated manner of dress, there is actually nothing about her on most occasions that would even lead anyone to believe that she is only spirit. Many witnesses have described meeting this poor soul and mistaking her for a young girl dressed in costume. Some have even described her as a bride due to the elaborate white dress. If only she had been able to be a bride. That would have perhaps avoided this entire terrible adventure and would have allowed this soul to find rest.

The Catholic Chapel. It sits directly across the street from the Morrison House on the corner of Washington Avenue and Stony Lonesome. It is the home to spirits of its own. A girl in a white dress is often seen walking along the edge of the upper balcony, but even more disturbing are those occasions when she is seen strolling through the air at a height that exceeds the spire on the church.

There is of course one instance when this apparition can certainly not be mistaken for a normal young girl or an expectant bride-to-be. That involves those disturbing sighting of this poor soul when she appears floating in the air. Not just a few inches above the ground as ghosts are often depicted as doing, but almost a hundred feet up in the air. She has been seen to walk in a small circle, as if she were on a lighthouse balcony. Back and forth, looking out to the horizon, clasping her hands, muttering to herself, and then, most tragically, the young girl steps away from her prescribed small circle, takes a step or two straight out, and then is seen to plummet straight down to the ground where she inevitably disappears.

The origins of this ghost go back to the turn of the century. In 1898, West Point had grown in size and had just over 500 cadets housed in the barracks on the post. This was a several hundred percent increase over the two hundred cadets who were students a mere forty years previously. The increase in students had warranted a corresponding growth across the academy. New academic buildings were being built, new library, new barracks. One of the new buildings that was completed during this time was an observatory. It was a large granite tower that was attached to the new library and extended almost a hundred feet into the sky.

In addition to the new buildings that were required on campus, there was a requirement for an increased number of instructors and professors at the academy. It happened that one of the new instructors had a young daughter. A beautiful young girl of 19, with warm pink skin, just a slight shade darker than most other girls of the area, and dark hair with an auburn tinge to it. Her appearance gave her an exotic look that instantly made her the object of many young cadet's fantasies and the envy of many of the local young girls. They pictured themselves in her position, living on the military campus, surrounded by young men who desired her for her beauty.

The reality of the situation was not quite so glamorous. Her father was a stern man. An instructor of math, he had lost his wife in childbirth and had dedicated his life to his daughter. He spent as much time shielding his daughter from the eyes of the young cadets as he did working on his numbers. His efforts, however, were pointless. When a beautiful girl lives among over 500 young men, there is no way to impede the pull that is stronger than the lunar-tides that flowed up the Hudson daily. A certain young cadet caught her eye and the two fell in love. The cadet had set himself a difficult task. Not only did he have to contend with the possible physical repercussions of the jealousy of some 900 of his classmates, but he also had to find a way to win over the stern math master.

The young cadet lost no opportunity to excel at his studies as a way to impress the instructor. He soon excelled at his studies and used this as an excuse to visit the math instructor on the pretext of procuring further directions of study. The math professor was not fooled by the cadet's new found enthusiasm for math but he appreciated his dedication and soon he began to soften his heart to the young man. He began to tutor the young man in his house after regular study hours and did not object too strenuously when his young daughter would bring them tea or bread and jam. In due course, he would even leave the study for a period of time "to find some book upstairs" and might not return to the study for the better part of half an hour, sometimes forgetting the book that he had supposedly gone to get in the first place.

The only time that they were ever actually "alone," was when the professor gave the couple the key to the observatory tower to allow them an opportunity to "study the night skies." These trips to the tower were the best moments of the young couple's time together. They would look through the telescope at distant worlds, stroll around the railed balcony at the top of the tower, and even on one or two occasions, steal a quick kiss. One of the young girl's favorite activities was when the two would sit with their legs dangling over the precipice below while the young cadet would read to her from Shakespeare. The poetry and plays of the bard became a staple part of their growing romance.

The relationship developed over the better course of a year and the young cadet was coming to a point where he was about to discuss with his parents the possibility of his asking this young woman to be his wife. This situation might have ended gloriously for everyone involved. The young cadet would have received his commission and his new bride within a matter of months. The young girl would have been lucky enough to find a boy she loved who also had the blessings of her parent. The math instructor would have had a pupil who was the most dedicated math student that he had ever encountered.

Scandal

It did not end gloriously, however. The ugly monster of jealousy reared its head and any pleasurable outcome that the fates had initially planned turned horribly tragic. Another local young girl who had set her sights on this same cadet became more and more enraged as she saw the relationship progress between the young couple. She plotted and planned and connived to find some way to ruin the relationship. At last an opportunity presented itself.

At a social function that was hosted by one of the more esteemed dowagers in the area, the two young girls, the cadet's beloved, and her rival, found themselves seated next to each other at the same table. The rival lost no time in making overtures of friendship to the professor's daughter and the two soon became inseparable. By all outward appearances, they were the best of friends, but inwardly the rival was plotting and biding her time. As the two grew more and more intimate, secrets were exchanged. The rival, of course, shared nothing that was real or of any consequence. The professor's daughter on the other hand, shared a secret that was bound to change her life. The secret to her shade-off skin tone and her exotic beauty lay in her heritage. Her father was a soldier, as had been her grandfather. Her grandfather had also been a soldier and had served in the Mexican-American War. After the U. S. had defeated Mexico and U. S. troops had occupied Mexico City, many of the elite families in the city had hosted the visiting officers. The U. S. officers had availed themselves of this hospitality in more ways than one. The professor's father had fallen in love with and had married a young Mexican girl who was the daughter of a wealthy merchant family. The money that had come to him through this marriage had allowed him to make the social connections necessary to allow opportunities for his son, such as attending West Point. Although the professor showed very little of his Mexican heritage, there was just enough of the lineage present in his daughter to make her stand out from the other girls of the area.

This was truly a scandalous secret for the time. Regardless of the fact that the wealthy Mexicans of that time were mostly Spanish and were just as European as any of the other residents of America, most people in "polite society" viewed Mexicans on the same level as they viewed Native Americans. Fine for a purpose, but hardly civilized enough to be called equals and certainly not the type that you wanted your children marrying.

It was an unfortunate circumstance that the cadet that loved the professor's daughter came from one of those Eastern families that would have viewed a marriage to a Mexican as unbearable. The rival knew this and so, through the use of a surreptitious third party, she let it be known to the mother of the cadet that this young lady was "one of those." The young cadet never stood a chance. Before he even had an opportunity to bring the matter up to his parents, his mother intervened and forbade him from seeing the young girl anymore. The young cadet did not know what to do. He had no intention of staying away from his beloved but he had been brought up to be a proper young man and it was difficult for him to conceive of going against his family's wishes. He visited the house of the professor and had a discussion with the older man about his desires and plans. The professor told the young man that he would not help him go against the wishes of his family, but neither would he stand in his way and actively prevent him from pursuing whatever goal he desired. With this turmoil roiling underneath the surface and indecision in the air, graduation came about.

At graduation, many cadets were surprised to find that their first assignment after receiving their commission would be to go to Cuba and the Philippines to fight in the just declared Spanish-American War. The young cadet, now a lieutenant, found himself being deployed before having a chance to resolve the situation between his love and his family.

He lost no time in writing to his love. Many of his letters would be reminiscences of their time together and would often be accompanied by quotes from Shakespeare. When the young girl received these letters, she lost no time in replying. Often she would go up to the top of the academy observatory and read the letters and stare up at the stars, while she composed her replies.

It did not take long after the deployment for the newly commissioned lieutenant to come to a reckoning regarding his situation. Two letters arrived at West Point at the end of the first month. One was written to the professor, asking the professor for permission to marry his daughter upon his return. The other was written to the young girl. In it he profusely professed his undying love to her. He told her that he had written a letter to his parents to inform them that he would be getting married upon his return, and that they could either welcome the event or despise it, but either way it would not sway his decision. He closed the letter by asking her forgiveness for not simply marrying her before he left, regardless of his parents opinions. He shared another quote from Shakespeare with her to express his feelings. He said that he had blamed his parents or her grandparents or social conditions for them not being joined in marriage already, but in truth he had no one to blame but himself. He sent the quote from Shakespeare's "Julius Caesar" where Brutus and Cassius are bewailing the fates for their situation and Cassius reminds Brutus that: "The fault, dear Brutus, lies not in our stars but in our selves."

"The fault is only mine, my dearest," he wrote, "And is not a twist of fate or the result of the alignment of stars in the sky. Upon my return, you and I will look up at the stars from our observatory and dare them to even try to stand between us."

The young girl cherished the letter and thought of nothing but the day when her young lieutenant would return. Immediately following this letter, however, a week passed with no letter. Then a second week passed. The young girl became frantic for word of her beloved lieutenant. She sought out her supposed new friend, the spiteful rival, and asked if she had heard anything from the family about the young man. She had not heard anything from the family since the last letter and was afraid of approaching them to ask them anything for fear that they were still adamantly set against her. She expressed the hope that her "friend" could serve as a liaison with the young man's family until some rapprochement had been achieved. The professor's daughter was so emotional at this point that she could no longer hold back the final secret to which she was clinging. She confessed to her supposed friend the plans for her and the lieutenant to marry when he returned and she begged her friend to help her obtain any word about her now-fiancee.

The rival became enraged and flew into a fury. She had thought that she had thwarted any possible chance of a lasting union between the two with her meddling. She had kept the other girl in the dark, however, just in case there was a need for a further intervention. Now that she saw the truth of the matter she let her true self be known. She began to mock the professor's daughter and began calling her nasty, derogatory names. She told her that it had been she who had let the mother know about her ancestral secret and had ruined their chance of being married before the lieutenant had deployed.

The loss of one she had thought of as a friend devastated the young girl. The rival saw the distraught and broken look on the girl's face and decided to play the final card in her wicked game. She told the young girl that the reason that she had not heard from her lieutenant in two weeks was because he had been killed in the fighting. He was dead and would never return to claim her as his bride.

Love Lost Forever

This was of course not true, but the poor young girl had no way of knowing this. She could not see this as simply one more in a series of lies. She was a good person herself and even after being faced with the truth of the rival's treachery, she still took the other girl's word at face value. She would have thought it the highest cruelty to tell such a lie and so would not expect it of others. In a totally distraught loss of her ability to think clearly, the young girl returned home and gathered up her letters from her soldier. She rushed to the observatory tower near the library and climbed up and up until she found herself out on the railing overlooking the campus and the valley beyond. It is not believed at this point that she had any conscious desire to end her life. It was simply that one place to which she would go to remind her of her lieutenant whom she now believed was lost to her forever.

No one knows if her plunge over the edge of the rail was a calculated thing or simply the unfocused meandering of a distraught mind. What they do know though is that her lifeless body was found at the base of the tower shortly after she fell. The letters from her love were found scattered around her with the exception of one. The last letter from her soldier was clutched in her hand with her finger poignantly poised over the line, "The fault, dear Brutus, lies not in our stars, but in ourselves."

The young soldier, who had not had the opportunity to send a letter home for a while was shocked to receive a letter from the professor one day, informing him that the young girl whom he had pledged to marry was now dead. In a fit of sorrow and rage, the lieutenant struck out on a charge that was fueled by nothing other than loss. He streaked across the lines with no thought of support to help him. He charged with no idea of what he would do if he achieved the other side of the lines. It was never necessary for him to find out, however, since he never made it to the other side. A Spanish rifle stopped his charge and his heartache all in one merciful moment. The jealousy of a dark heart had now cost two lives.

The mathematics professor also found his heart broken. He had lost his wife with the birth of his daughter, and since then, he had lived only for his daughter. Now that she was gone, his life was little more than a hollow shell. He resigned his commission in the Army and moved out west to teach and was never heard from again.

The Haunting

The haunting of the observatory began almost immediately. Cadets began reporting seeing an image of a young girl in a white dress walking around the top of the observatory and then seeing her plunge down to the paving stones below. Emergency calls went out one after another until they realized that this plunge was nothing more than the repetitive actions of a restless spirit.

In the 1920s, the old library was torn down to make way for a new library and the observatory that was attached to it was moved to the top of Lusk. It was thought at the time that moving the monstrous structure might end the repetition of the doomed fall of the young girl but it did not. Still, most were satisfied that at least the observatory was out of the cadet area now and the sightings would be less distracting. Certainly it was for the cadets but not for the residents of Lusk that now observed this phenomenon at least a few times a year.

Within a few years, however, even these sightings began to decrease as the observatory ceased to be utilized. For twenty years the monolith stood empty, jutting out into the night sky, silhouetted by the absence of stars behind its mass. With few cadets journeying up to the observatory for class and only a handful of families living on the hilltop, the spirit was almost forgotten for a time.

That was until 1957. In that year the Catholic Chapel on West Point wanted to extend their facility by building a rectory and a new balcony. They had the funds for it and were ready to do it all without any government assistance. There was one small hitch, however. Due to the historic nature of the post, any renovations that occur on West Point have to be approved by the post historian and the post architect and must meet certain guidelines. One of the rules about renovating or extending old buildings was that the building must present a uniform appearance when complete. In most cases, this meant using weathered granite that closely matched the appearance of the granite already in use on the structure. For the Catholic Chapel, however, this was a problem. The quarry that had been used to supply the stone for the chapel was no longer in use. The stone had mostly been exhausted.

Then the parish priest on post had a brilliant idea. The stone that had been used for the observatory had been taken from the same quarry and was very similar in appearance to the stone of the chapel. He hatched the ingenious plan of buying the old observatory and using the stone for the new construction. Since this was a government building, West Point wound up putting the observatory up for auction, with the highest bidder responsible for the demolition and removal of the structure. The Catholic Chapel was the highest, and only, bidder and purchased the old structure for the grand sum of one dollar. Over the course of the next five years, the observatory was slowly taken apart piece by piece. For five years, there were no more sightings of the girl in white and her ten-story plunge.

In 1962, the new addition to the chapel was complete and a dedication service was held. The parish priest was surprised to find a young girl hanging around after all of the festivities were complete. She seemed oddly dressed and he wondered if perhaps she were a bride that had come to the Catholic Chapel instead of the Cadet Chapel further up the hill by mistake. He approached her to find out what she was doing there but as he drew close, she simply disappeared. This began a new series of sightings of the girl in white.

Since that day she is still seen. Often simply hanging out, walking around the new additions of the church, looking just like any other young girl, except for her out-of-date white dress and her haunting beauty.

The oldest section of the West Point cemetery. The grave in the center of the photo marked "Unknown" is reportedly the grave of Tioran O'Connor.

8
The Irish Apparition

No story of ghosts would be complete without a visit to the grave yard. The question at West Point is, which ghost in the grave yard to focus on. Many of the graves at the West Point cemetery have spirits associated with them. Because of the violent nature of the business soldiers are inherently involved in, many of the souls interred there are restless or passed suddenly leaving unfinished business. In many of the cases, however, the spirit is little more than a graveyard myth and the apparitions are completely unverified. There are enough verified hauntings at West Point, though, that we can choose at our leisure from the verified cases.

Saved by the Bell

The most obvious one, and the one with perhaps the most verified sightings, would be the ghost of Viele (pronounced *vee-lee*). Viele was a West Point graduate, as well as the chief engineer for Central Park in Manhattan and Prospect Park in Brooklyn, and a U. S. Representative from New York. He also was deathly afraid of being buried alive. (This fear was shared by a previous West Point cadet, the famous poet, Edgar Allan Poe.) Viele was so frightened of being buried alive that he stipulated that his grave was to be outfitted with a buzzer that would ring a bell in the superintendent's house should Viele find himself prematurely interred. (Oddly enough, this buzzer was one of the first uses of electricity at the Point.) Over the years, this buzzer sounded so many times that the superintendent eventually had it dismantled. The initial explanations were faulty wiring or pranks by cadets, but the numerous sightings of the old engineer cast doubt on these logical explanations.

Tioran O'Connor

The most interesting ghost story at the West Point cemetery, however, is perhaps the story of Tioran O'Connor. This is also the one with the most recent and public report.

About the Cemetery

It is necessary to understand a bit about the West Point cemetery before we go further into this story or much of the story may not make sense. The cemetery itself was officially established in 1817, but people had been buried in that spot prior to the official dedication. There were also several individual gravesites scattered around the area that the post covered. These graves were located and moved to the newly dedicated site. As the fort grew and construction took place, additional graves were discovered and each one was moved. This oldest portion of the cemetery takes up the southeastern corner of the graveyard. The graves there are placed in ever widening semi-circles that look out toward the Hudson River. Starting sometime in the 1860s, possibly due to the increased number of deceased West Point graduates from the Civil War, the semi-circle configuration was changed to the more traditional (and more space-efficient) method of lines and rows. This arrangement makes it fairly easy to get a rough estimate of the time period in which a person died by the section of the graveyard in which they are buried.

There are two buildings in the cemetery, aside from the mausoleums. One is the Old Cadet Chapel that was built on the plain in 1836 and was moved to the cemetery in 1911 to make room for new construction. The other is only slightly more recent, a house that was originally built as a home for the caretaker, but is now no longer lived in.

The Ceremony

Most of the ceremonies and services take place in or near the Old Cadet Chapel. Every now and then they will hold a service in the northwestern corner where most of the new burials of graduates who were killed in Iraq or Afghanistan take place. Occasionally, there will be some special event that takes place at the grave of Margaret Corbin, the original Molly Pitcher, on the side of the chapel. Rarely, however, is there ever a ceremony in the old section of the cemetery, where the semi-circular lines of stones seem to reach out like arms to embrace anyone standing in their midst.

One of these rare ceremonies occurred on Veteran's Day in 2008. It is customary to hold Veteran's Day memorial services at military bases and West Point is no different. In 2008, a Veteran's Day service was scheduled to be held and the officer in charge recommended that they hold it in the old section of the cemetery. The recommendation was approved. Four days prior to the event, the honor guard began rehearsing for the ceremony. The first two practice runs were conducted in the North Area of the cadet barracks. The day prior to the event, the rehearsal was scheduled to be held on site at the cemetery.

The honor guard reported oddities from the time they arrived on the site. Almost immediately the professionally trained guard who had conducted numerous similar exercises was uncustomarily dropping weapons and becoming confused about the order of the events. At least two of the five members of the honor guard got pretty severe bruises from accidentally kicking their shins and knees against headstones when they inexplicably lost their balance. The mishaps culminated when one of the rifles being used for practice actually fired a live round instead of a blank.

Two things are clear from the report. The officer in charge of the detail testified that he had personally inspected each weapon, as was routine. Each of the members of the detail reported that they had also inspected their weapons and verified that the captain had done so too. And yet the fact remained that the weapon being used by SGT Morris had fired. When the chamber was inspected, a spent, live round was found in it. The captain of the guard immediately thought that SGT Morris had smuggled in the round as some sort of a practical joke. He fired him from the squad and sent him back to the barracks. It was his intention to punish him under the UCMJ (Uniform Code of Military Justice) had the following events not transpired.

After dismissing SGT Morris, the captain continued the rehearsal. On the very next run through, the rifle belonging to SSG Thomas also fired. Another inspection of the weapon revealed another expended, live cartridge. The captain now assumed that either the entire team was in on the joke or one person was sabotaging the others. He found it unlikely that it was a collaboration since it was very clear that he intended to press charges against the offenders. This meant that it was more likely one person intentionally causing problems. Since SGT Morris was not there for the second incident, it now seemed likely that at least he was innocent. Of the other four men, the captain would have sworn that none of them were likely to do such a thing, yet it had to be one of them.

The captain told the remaining four soldiers that if someone came clean and admitted to the prank, he would recommend only a company grade punishment with minimal actual punishment, but if no one owned up to it he would have no choice but to call in the MPs and then the charges would be much more severe. No one came forward and so the captain called in the MPs.

The MPs arrived and initiated an investigation. The results would not be known until ten days later. The investigation determined that a person or persons unknown had intentionally tampered with and switched out the live ammo. They could find no time, however, when this could have been accomplished based on the corroborating statements of all those involved. Additionally, they found no fingerprints on the second casing and only the captain's fingerprints on the first round, which was accounted for when he took the round out of the chamber. As if that were not enough, all men passed a bio-metric lie detection test, which is even more accurate than a polygraph. The conclusion was that it had to be one of the detail but that it couldn't have been one of the detail.

Meanwhile, the ceremony still had to go forward. A second detail was assigned and quickly trained but since the captain had been involved in making statements, they were not able to rehearse on site at the time. They did run-throughs in the MP area though. Early in the morning, the captain took them to the graveyard to attempt another live run through. As they took their places, one of the replacements tripped and fell, severely injuring his ankle. He had to be taken to the hospital where it was discovered that he had broken his ankle. Another replacement had to be located and quickly schooled on firing ceremonies. They did not have any time for a full run through and the captain was mostly hoping that he could simply get through the ceremony without seriously embarrassing himself.

This time all of the blank ammunition was double and triple checked. An MP and a colonel also independently verified that the ammunition was blank and the weapons were not messed with. Additionally, the captain made all of the soldiers in the detail empty their pockets, just in case.

The speeches were made and the rifle squad prepared to fire. They aimed into the air at the tree line and fired. It was immediately obvious that live rounds had been fired. The sound of the explosion and the zing through the air signaled that something was dreadfully amiss. As if to add an exclamation point to the mishap, a cracking sound from above signaled that at least one of the rounds had struck a tree branch. The damaged branch creaked in protest for a moment and then fell to the ground below with a dramatic splintering, striking a civilian female attendee. She also wound up going to the hospital and received three stitches along the edge of her hairline.

The captain wisely chose not to fire the remaining two volleys and frantically whispered to the bugler to begin playing "Taps." As several people attended the wounded woman and called for help, the bugler blew the first note of "Taps." That was all he got out. A violent fit of coughing seized him and would not stop until the colonel who was overseeing the ceremony tried to announce, as graciously as possible, an end to the event.

MPs were already on the scene at the event and an immediate inspection of the rifles was conducted which resulted in the discovery of five spent cartridges from live rounds. The branch that had fallen was examined and evidence that three of the rounds had struck the branch were found. Once again, after a lengthy investigation and more lie detector tests, it was determined that what had happened was simply not possible.

In and Out the Door

This unexplainable event might have faded away and never found its way to the "Way Out There" Internet news sites as it did, had it not been for the fact that the colonel in charge of the ceremony was a history professor. The situation was so odd that he felt it needed further investigation. While searching the archives of the library, he came across a small scrap of an article intimating a similar event had occurred a little more than forty years earlier. That small story, itself referenced an even earlier event that was mentioned as having occurred in 1893. There were almost no details given about the incidents but using the research techniques that all good historians command, he was able to eventually find the name of an individual who had been convicted at court martial for "endangering lives" in the 1965 incident. The man in question had been dishonorably discharged. The colonel was able to locate the man, almost seventy now. Initially, he was reluctant to speak about an incident that he still held a lot of bitterness about, but eventually he conceded.

After he began talking, it seemed almost as if he was grateful to get it off his chest. As he related the story, it seemed identical to what had most recently transpired. Constant accidents and mishaps, culminating in the firing of live rounds. Although they could not prove anything, the investigators knew that such a thing could not have happened without outside intervention, so the blame was eventually placed on him.

That might have been the end of the story, had not the old man muttered, "I should have listened to the old man," as the colonel got up to go. This throw-away remark was what many interviewers and psychologists call: "the question in the door." It is that thing about which the person being spoken to wishes to talk about but is reluctant to. Nevertheless, they cannot let the opportunity pass and will wait until their questioner is "in the door" to bring up the real issue. The colonel immediately asked the man to elaborate as to what he meant by saying that he should have listened to the old man. Thus, the rest of the tale came out. It seemed that an old groundskeeper had seen the preparations for the ceremony and had warned against it. When the man the colonel was questioning had queried the groundskeeper about why the ceremony should not take place, the groundskeeper related an earlier tragic event and an unheeded warning from an old sergeant. That sergeant reported an even earlier mishap and a warning from a local newspaperman. And so it went back, incident after incident, unheeded warning after unheeded warning, stretching all the way back for over 140 years.

A Beast Waiting to be Released

It seems that the genesis of the story began shortly after the Civil War. Many Civil War officers on both sides of the war were West Point graduates and in fact by the end of the war, every single general officer was a graduate of the academy. One young officer, a lieutenant by the name of Tioran O'Connor, was a graduate of the academy and served with a much older academy graduate, one Ulysses S. Grant.

The two officers hit it off almost immediately. They were both very opinionated men and neither one ever hesitated to speak their minds. It was not long before Tioran shared with the general one of his deepest concerns. He had severe misgivings regarding the legality of the endeavor in which they were engaged. He was an adamant abolitionist and passionately disagreed with the south's contention that slavery was a legitimate practice, but he was uncertain as to whether or not the government had the right to go to war to enforce this issue.

It turned out that Ulysses S. Grant was just the one that he could go to with these concerns. Grant himself, that great general and eventual president of the country, had once had the very same concerns regarding the United States involvement in the War with Mexico. Grant had felt that the actions of the United States had less to do with national security and more to do with the fledgling nations need to flex its imperial power over a smaller, weaker neighbor. Grant had gone so far as to write letters against the war while at the same time serving in the war with distinction. Through counseling with this kindred spirit, Tioran was able to find peace with his stance on the war but he was never quite able to reconcile himself with the violent side of his profession that he was often faced with.

Tioran wrote to relatives that the "just face of the war could not hide the hideous visage of necessary violence that lurked just below the surface as some beast waiting to be released." Tioran saw the face of the beast on more than a few occasions. On one such occasion he was instrumental in stopping the rape and pillaging of a southern homestead by Union soldiers who had forgotten their better selves and had given full power to their baser natures. They had released the beast within themselves and Tioran had stood up against their tyranny. He had saved the homestead and the mother and her two girls but had gotten wounded severely in the leg in the process.

He would go on to recover and would once again face the beast when other soldiers went on a rampage during the sack of Vicksburg. This time, they were fellow officers who swore after the fact that they had done no wrong and that Tioran was nothing more than a southern sympathizer. It was only his noted bravery during the siege and his personal friendship with General Grant that wound up saving him from getting a court martial for standing up for what he knew was right. In the end, he became bitter and cynical about the profession that he had chosen. He wished to leave the violence of arms behind him but could not do so with a clean conscience while the war was still raging. It turned out that both his life and the war would come to almost simultaneous ends.

In one of the final conflicts of the war, Tioran was injured once again in the leg where he had received his previous injury. This necessitated that his leg be amputated. The survival odds of a battlefield amputation were slim at the time, but Tioran was able to beat those odds. He would live to see the end of the war but the leg never healed properly. Infection set in that Tioran had difficulty fighting off. He lasted until April 17th, the day after Lincoln was assassinated. It seemed that this final violent act of a war that had so stolen his many high ideals was the last straw. He was unable to go on fighting and the infection finally took him.

The country was fractured at this point. The new president was sworn in and was faced with the difficulty of running a nation that had been held together at the cost of half a million lives. Fundamentally, the ideologies had not changed. The two sides were still bitterly opposed. The only difference was that they lacked the ability to continue the conflict on a martial footing. The new administration sought valiantly for anything that they could find that could help bind the two sides back to a functioning whole. One of the many programs that were enacted at this time was the aggrandizement of heroes, or the creation of them out of whole cloth if necessary. They hoped that they could rally people around individuals who represented the best that both sides had to offer. Individuals were sought who could be given awards and medals in public forums and who could find a broad appeal.

During this search, the story of Tioran O'Connor came out. Someone remembered his bravery against Union soldiers during the plantation incident and even his ability to stand up against his own brother officers during the Vicksburg sack. His unimpeachable credentials for bravery and his willingness to defend a southerner when it was the right thing to do made him the perfect candidate for this campaign. Unfortunately, he was already dead. The bureaucrats, however, hit upon a plan that they thought was perfect. They would disinter the soldier from his cemetery on Long Island and reinter him with much pomp and ceremony at the cemetery in West Point. An example like Tioran would be used to show the south that northerners too cared about them and would fight for their rights just as they did for all citizens.

One of the big problems with this plan, aside from the general hyperbolic hypocrisy, was that as a West Point graduate, Tioran had been offered the opportunity to be buried at West Point already and had steadfastly refused. He had stated over and over again in letters to family and friends that he wished to be buried in his local community cemetery should anything befall him and wished no part in continuing his eternal memory with that profession that he grew to despise. When the infection in his leg had grown and death had seemed imminent, he had repeated this request over and over again. Many people considered being buried at West Point a great honor and he wanted to ensure that his last wishes were understood.

Initially, his family objected to the plan to reinter Tioran at West Point, however, after some patriotic cajoling and some promises of cash were made, they finally consented. The arrangements were made and the grand ceremony took place. It seemed almost from the very beginning that the spirit of the soldier-turned-pacifist was enraged to his once warrior state. Troubles plagued the initial ceremony just as they had the Veteran's Day celebration. In this case, however, the results were even more tragic. The event was attended by a rather large crowd. A contingent of the press, members of congress, officers from both sides of the conflict, and citizenry desperate for a celebration came along for the show.

Along with the dropped rifles and stubbed toes and malfunctioning equipment was another series of misfires. This time, however, there was no shattered branch that would require a few stitches. Instead, there was a startled cart horse that bolted from its place and headed off down the crowded path. Most of the party-goers were panicked but managed to get out of the way. A few were knocked over and bruised, but that would have been considered preferable over what eventually happened. A young girl, about five years old, had wandered away from her mother's hand towards the edge of the road to get a better view of the festivities. Her attention was still drawn to events that were going on across the street when the horse lost control. She was totally oblivious to the catastrophe hurtling towards her. Her mother had only just come to the realization that her child was no longer holding her hand when she saw the out-of-control horse and buggy.

The child died immediately upon impact. The festivities died with her. The good idea had not only desecrated the last wishes of a soldier but had also taken the life of a young girl in the process. The headstone that they had scheduled to put up over Tioran's grave seemed almost obscene after the tragedy that had occurred. Instead, it was replaced with a simple headstone marked "Unknown" as if the entire incident could be erased by refusing to acknowledge the name of the soldier who rested there.

Since that first tragic moment, no ceremony has gone off at that location without some catastrophe accompanying it. There have been no further fatalities associated with that area, but countless injuries. It is such an idyllic location. It is the oldest portion of the cemetery and also houses the cadet memorial which lists the names of all cadets who have died while attending the academy. Famous residents of that area of the cemetery include, among others, the Warner sisters, composers of the famous children's tune "Jesus Loves Me." It calls out to be used and remembered. But those who know, never will. About every thirty to forty years or so, the memories fade and a ceremony is scheduled. A memorial or a celebration or a photo -op is planned, rehearsed, and carried out to varying degrees of success, and inevitably, someone limps away. Inevitably, there is always someone older and disregarded who stands in the background and says, "I told you so."

A Visit from Tioran

The spirit of Tioran O'Connor that haunts that area of the cemetery has no tolerance for pomp and circumstance. He views it as part and parcel of the reason that his physical remains are interred in a cemetery that he despises. There are two other things that are sure to bring about a visit from the restless spirit.

The first is any type of weapon. His enmity towards instruments of violence is not solely limited to those that are used in ceremonial functions. Before regulations forbid such things, anyone who happened to travel into that area carrying a gun often suffered embarrassing and even painful repercussions. Guns went off without triggers being pulled. Sometimes they would get painfully hot and have to be dropped on the ground. On one or two occasions, the guns simply fell apart.

Secondly, other weapons also fall victim to these machinations. Any type of metal weapon such as a knife or sword of any kind would inexplicably heat up until it could no longer be touched. Sometimes this would require them to be dropped to the ground and kicked with a shoe until it was out of the area of Tioran's influence. Kids wandering through the area and playing with slingshots would find that the stone or metal missiles fired from their usually harmless toys would almost always find a way to ricochet back and leave a welt on a cheek or any unprotected surface of the skin.

The third way that one can guarantee himself or herself a visit from the spirit would be to travel to that area of the graveyard with any deep-seated anger or hatred dwelling in their soul. Tioran viewed the hearts of man as being more dangerous than any weapon that they may or may not carry since it was these emotions that brought a great nation to fight against itself and lose over a half a million of its fathers and sons in needless slaughter. It was these emotions that took countless more through random acts of violence that were facilitated by the war but not required of it. Depending on the degree of enmity held in one's soul, a visit to the cemetery might generate a feeling of sorrow or utter despair. Tears would stream unbidden from the most callous of individuals if they failed to resolve their conflicts before wandering through that back area. For those more died-in-the-wool haters, there were even reports of the individual being knocked physically to the ground or thrown back hard enough to skin knees and elbows and bloody noses.

In addition to the attacks on ceremonies, weapons, and dark emotions that occur in this area of the cemetery, another sign of the presence of the spirit of Tioran O'Connor are the images seen by visitors to the cemetery. Since it is one of the prime stops on the tourist route through the academy, there are literally hundreds of visitors a day to the cemetery and inevitably one or two of them make their way back to the older section. Many of those who have walked through that portion of the graveyard have returned to their tour group and asked what reenactments are taking place in the cemetery that day. They report seeing a young man, about 24 or 25 years old, dressed in a uniform of the style that was worn during the Civil War, standing morosely and staring off into the distance, or sitting forlornly on a stone marked "Unknown."

These reports are always met with wonder by tour guides who might be new to the area. A follow-up visit to the area usually results in the tourist insisting that they saw something. Older, more seasoned tour guides simply nod and tell their guest that they have just seen the ghost of Tioran O'Connor. They tell the tourists that if nothing ugly happened to them that they must be a nice person and were judged to have a heart with no ill-will in it.

Sometimes these sightings report a figure of a small girl of about 5 or 6 that is standing or sitting with the soldier. It is almost certainly the spirit of the young girl that was lost in that first tragic horse and carriage incident. Many more visitors, who do not actually see the spirits while at the cemetery, have gone on to return to their homes only to develop their film and find the images of the soldier and the young girl superimposed over the pictures that they thought that they were taking.

The officer who originally investigated the latest incident has been back to the area on many occasions. On one of those occasions, he had forgotten to remove a pocketknife from his pants pocket and was fortunate that there was no one around to see him dance and jump away from the area while simultaneously unbuckling his pants. He attempted to reach into his pocket and remove the knife that had suddenly become red hot but could not touch it and so resorted to loosening his pants and holding the waist out around his knees so that the knife was safely suspended away from his skin. It left a nasty red scar on his thigh, but the mark that was even more enduring was the indelible spot that it burned into his memory. It has reminded him to always be conscious of the weapons that we carry, but even more so to be aware of the emotions that we carry in our hearts.

The area that lies just within the back gate of West Point at the entrance to the Stony Lonesome Pass. It is these barren and isolated ruins that gave the pass its name.

9
Stony Lonesome

When attempting to understand the various haunted locations around West Point, it is important to remember the chronological development of the post's boundaries. When it was founded in 1778, it was an area that encompassed six forts, several defensive cannon emplacements, and a few civilian residential areas. It was not incorporated as one single entity with a clearly defined boundary. The boundaries developed over time. The site that once held an artillery position, but now holds a gas station, may have at one time in the past been the site of a small farm. In fact, at one point or another, at least five different families had homes or farms on the area that now comprises the West Point main garrison area. One of those families was actually still making claims against land that the fort had claimed illegally and had not paid for up until the 1830s. It is not uncommon for new construction projects to uncover not only evidence of earlier military dwellings but also of civilian homesteads.

The single largest collection of these former dwellings dates back to well before the time that the fort was formed. The ruins of an entire community lie just inside the post boundaries near the Stony Lonesome gate. The remains of this abandoned village consist of over twenty homes and various structures. The skeletal remains of these old buildings also hold the largest single concentration of spirits at any location on West Point, with the exception of perhaps the cemetery. This is the story of how that village came to be, how it came to be abandoned, and how over 130 souls came to be doomed to wander those empty streets forever.

The Cathar Overshadowed

The time between Hudson's discovery of the area that became West Point in 1609 and the time that the area became instrumental in the birth of a new nation in 1776, there were 167 years when different nations vied for control of the area. Many attempts were made to exploit it for its wealth of furs and timber. Several attempts were made to colonize the area for the sake of one empire or another. The Dutch, the French, the Danes, and eventually the English, all tried to make the area part of their greater empire. There were, however, smaller, less extrinsically motivated groups that attempted to start new colonies in the area. One group of Scots traveled to the area during the period when control was in flux between the Dutch and the French. They were not trying to extend a Scottish empire, they were simply trying to start a new life, away from the injustices that they experienced at the hands of the British. Their settlement was unsuccessful but their dreams were eventually realized in the American Revolution.

Another of these lesser known groups that traveled to the area during this time, when everything past a mile inland was frontier, was a small group of Spanish Cathar missionaries. The Cathars were a very strict, very fanatical sect of Christians who had begun in the Languedoc region of France but had been hunted almost to extinction during the Albigensian crusade of Pope Innocent the III. The few survivors of this sect continued teaching their beliefs but their believers were few in number. During outbreaks of war, famine, or plague, these extremists would increase in numbers as the down-trodden would turn to them to explain why God had abandoned them. Once the tragedy passed, however, the converts would return to their previous ways.

In the early 1600s, there was another outbreak of plague in parts of Europe. One of the harder hit areas was the coastal region of Spain. A Cathar priest, that many viewed as a mad man, came down from the Basque mountain regions and began to preach the Cathar ways among the panicked population. Scores of the fearful flocked to the Cathar faith. The rush became even more rapid when it was reported that this Cathar priest had actually healed people who were afflicted with the plague. This revitalization of the Cathar faith became so great that the Spanish royalty, who were at war with France but were actually still related to those same French noblemen who had persecuted the Cathars 300 years earlier, launched their own campaign against the newly strengthened faith.

The Cathar priest became concerned that his rapidly growing flock would wind up being put to death or forced to convert. He decided that the best course of action was to take his people somewhere where governments did not have the ability to control people's religious desires. It was also his desire to get his people away from the plague-ridden cities of Spain since he viewed the disease as a judgment of God. Since one of the tenets of the Cathar faith was poverty, it was very easy for the priest to get new converts to turn over all of their worldly goods to him. Most converts had no worldly goods to speak of since he preached among the homeless and the poor, but there were still one or two merchants and nobleman who had converted. They had contributed fairly substantial funds to the Cathar treasury. To his credit, the Cathar priest practiced what he preached and made no effort keep any money for himself, but instead made sure that it went to help the poor and needy. There was still enough money available, however, that he was able to outfit three ships. These three ships were commissioned to take 280 passengers to the new world—what the priest hoped would be the promised land. It was their intention to start a new settlement far away from the interference of the Spanish king and to begin mission work among the natives who lived in the new land.

Antonio de Sotomayor was the Royal Confessor, Archbishop of Damascus, and Spain's Inquisitor General at the time. He was an austere and unforgiving man but by all accounts was at least sincere. He was one of the key instigators of the internal crusade against the Cathars. Too late, he found out about the commissioning of the ships. As he rushed down to the docks, he arrived just in time to see the three ships clearing the mouth of the Spanish port. In anger, Sotomayor called for one of his servant priests to bring him a pyx with holy Eucharist in it. The Archbishop lifted up the body of Christ and prayed that God would smite the ships before they reached their destination. He then took the bread and consumed it. Almost immediately, witnesses said that the Archbishop fell down and suffered a stroke. Not only was half of his face paralyzed, but the skin itself was darkened. It is theorized that because the archbishop had used the holy bread of communion to call down a curse from God, the act had rebounded on him and had struck him as an invalid. The result was that Sotomayor became one of the least violent Inquisitor Generals from that point on, until his death a dozen years later.

The other thing, however, that witnesses reported, in addition to the stroke, is that as Sotomayor fell to the dock, a dark shadow seemed to pass out of him and glide through the water towards the departing ships. It is believed by some that this is the curse that continued to plague them for the short time that they had remaining here on earth.

An Ocean Voyage

It seemed that it would not take long for the curse to take effect. The ship's watch reported that for days they were being followed by a dark shadow in the water. At first it appeared as a faint discoloration in the distance. As it drew closer, it was assumed that it was possibly a whale, although why a whale would follow a ship, they could not surmise. The whale theory seemed to be born out, when on the fourth day out, the shadow drew close to the stern of the trail ship and the ship was rocked violently as if it had been struck by something. It was a hard enough hit that a few seams between the timbers sprung leaks and had to be repaired.

After the strike on one of the ships, the shadow in the water seemed to be replaced by a shadow in the sky. A cloud on the horizon seemed to take on an ashen stain. It was distinctly not a storm cloud. It seemed like a regular white cloud over which a large pall had been cast. The cloud sped towards them and soon a storm struck the three ships. For days, the ships were tossed about on monstrous waves and were struck by lightning more than once. In the middle of the fiercest part of the storm, one of the ships sunk. Only a handful of survivors made it into boats to be rescued by the two other ships. Most of the individuals on board the ship went down to the bottom of the sea. One of the other ships, the one that had been struck by the supposed whale, was severely damaged by the storm. Fortunately, by this time, they were within days of the new port city of New Amsterdam. They kept plugging leaks and bailing water until they arrived at the settlement of New Amsterdam and docked. They had neither the supplies nor the funds to repair their failing ship and so the priest ordered all of the people and belongings onto one ship.

It was fortunate at this time that some of the passengers decided to abandon the mission at this point and settle in the town of New Amsterdam. They had already had enough misfortune aboard the ships and had no desire to climb onto an even more cramped and overburdened ship to continue the voyage. The one remaining heavily laden ship then sailed on up the Hudson River. As they arrived near the area where Henry Hudson had once put ashore, the ship that had suffered through the storm at sea and was now severely overtaxed, began to give up the ghost and spring excessive leaks just like the other ship that they had left behind in New Amsterdam. The ship had to put in at the only marginally acceptable anchorage that presented itself. They settled the ship as close to the shore of Constitution Island (known at the time as Martelaer's Rock) as they could and began to unload the people and the supplies. After the ship was completely unloaded, they began to take apart and salvage as much of the lumber and riggings from the ship as they could. They did a fair amount of salvage work before the ship finally succumbed to the leaks and the ship slid beneath the water.

Settling In

They began their settlement on what seemed to be a promising site. They began to clear lumber and construct houses when once again, the shadow appeared. This time, it appeared out of a bright blue sky, drifting low over the tops of the trees. It was thought at first that it might be smoke from a fire, although no one had seen any sign of other inhabitants of the area. It moved so slowly, though, that no one was quite sure what to think about it. Just as the sun began to set, the shadow arrived and descended on the people below. They reported that they were stung and bitten by the largest cloud of mosquitoes or gnats that any of them had ever seen. All throughout the night they suffered, and by morning, most of them were covered in welts and sores from the attack. It is interesting to note, however, that no one actually ever reported seeing any insects. All they reported was the bites and stings. It is almost inconceivable that a swarm that large could have tortured them for so long without at least a few insect bodies being smashed and identified, but that is what they said.

The priest decided that the insects must have come from the marshy area that covered the eastern side of the island. Having just come from an area of plague it would make sense that they would want to distance themselves from an area that was often associated with insects and illness. With many aches and pains, a little regret, but just as much relief, they began the laborious task of moving their entire camp over to the far shore of the Hudson. They spent the next two days rowing the long boats back and forth, until all of their supplies were now perched on the narrow shore below the site where the town of Highland Falls stands today. This move also brought about their first casualty in their new homeland. One of the children who had been brought along on the journey began to run a fever and showed signs of serious infection from the multiple insect bites that he had suffered. By the time they had moved to the new camp he had passed away.

Their numbers now stood at just over 200 as they settled into their new location. The close proximity to the river offered them both food and water so their transition held the promise of being an easy one. This would not last long. The Hudson River, also known as "The River that Flows Both Ways," has a strong estuary flow. When heavy rains from upstream meet up with a heavy tide from the coast, the end result is often localized shoreline flooding. This was the case on the second day of the settlers attempt to start a new home. The heavy flow hit them just before first light when most of the settlers were still sleeping. Two people were simply washed away, as were a few of their belongings. Several more were soaked to the skin and only barely managed to escape being taken by the river. One of those developed an infection in the lung that turned into pneumonia and he died within a matter of days. The lookout who had been on guard duty that morning reported that he had seen a silvery gray shadow sliding down the river toward them just at the moment when the flood occurred, but most wrote that off as merely the movement of the water or a trick of the light.

The Cathar priest decided once again to move his followers. This time they moved up the hill, away from the river's edge. On the bluff overlooking the river, they still had access to the water and fish. Not as easy as if they were on the shore but it mitigated the risk that potential floods held. They began to settle in once again but again that only lasted a few days. After just over a week on the bluff, a landslide hit the bluff upon which they were living. Again, it cost them the lives of a few of their people as they tumbled off the bluff along with tons of dirt and rock and cascaded into the river below. And again, a gray shadow was reported as sliding over the ground toward them just before the tragedy struck.

The priest decided once again to move his followers. By this time many of them were grumbling and were less enthusiastic about their decision to leave Europe behind. With a few comments about Moses and the Israelites, however, the priest was able to bring everyone into line and they moved yet again. This time they built further inland and examined the area thoroughly for any potential hazards before beginning to settle in. It was at that point that the shadows began to get personal. No great tragedies struck, but individuals continued to suffer bizarre and consequential accidents. It was easy to explain away any singular event as nothing more than a coincidence, but the sheer mass of accidental falls, lost tools, spoiled food, and everything else that occurred, along with the ever present report of strange shadows, made it next to impossible to believe that there was not something directed specifically against them. And although no single tragedy struck the entire community at once, it did seem that a week could not go by without one of their number being laid to rest. A man was killed by a pack of wolves while coming home at night after a long day of hunting. A woman was crushed to death when a tree collapsed on her. Another woman simply tripped and fell and never got up again.

It seemed at least for a while that things might begin to achieve some sense of normalcy even with the deaths. A few random settlers and trappers wandered through the area and said that the new colonists

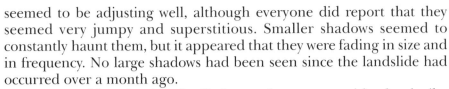

seemed to be adjusting well, although everyone did report that they seemed very jumpy and superstitious. Smaller shadows seemed to constantly haunt them, but it appeared that they were fading in size and in frequency. No large shadows had been seen since the landslide had occurred over a month ago.

It was at this point that the Cathar settlers met up with a local tribe of the Mahican natives. Suddenly, a new fervor swept through the Cathar settlement. Here they were living in their new land and now they were going to get a chance to preach without being persecuted for their beliefs. They were overjoyed. The Mahicans were very amenable to the new settlers coming over to their camp and speaking to them at first. It did not take long, however, for the avid Cathar priest to learn enough of the Mahican language to really anger them. He would come over with his followers and rail against the Mahican's pagan practices of worshiping spirits in the sky or the earth. He would become wide-eyed with passion as he spoke of the Cathars dualistic version of blended Christianity and how it was the only way to save the souls of the Mahicans. The Mahicans became less and less sociable to the Cathars as the priest became more and more virulent in his tirades.

The situation was already on the verge of becoming unstable when real tragedy struck. The Cathar missionaries arrived at the Mahican camp only to find out that a sickness had begun to spread among the natives. The first victim of this strange disease was brought before them and they recoiled in horror at what they saw. The large dark splotches on the face, the discoloration on the arms and legs, the swollen protuberances on the neck and in the armpits was terrifyingly familiar to them. It was the plague that they had crossed an ocean to avoid. The Cathars returned to their camp and left the natives to deal with this deadly outbreak. The priest held day long services where he preached against the sins of the Europeans whom they had just left and the sins of the pagans whom they had just met. For several days almost no work was done as the entire group prayed almost non-stop.

A New Curse

Three days later, as the sun was setting, a lone Mahican figure entered the edge of the camp and stood on a rise overlooking the area that the Cathar settlers had cleared. It was the Mahican shaman who faced them across the clearing. The Cathars looked gaunt and crazed as the shaman raised his hands above his head and let out a long cry. Then he began to pronounce a curse on the settlers. The Cathars below him only understood a little of what he was saying, but it was clear to their limited understanding of the Mahican language that the curse he was uttering was truly terrible in nature. It seemed that the plague that had started in the village was of a particularly virulent and contagious breed. The entire Mahican settlement had been wiped out. The shaman was the last survivor of the tribe and he issued forth the most dire threats and curses that he could muster on those that he blamed for his people's tragic death. Then it seemed that a gray cloud descended around him and the shaman simply disappeared into the growing night.

This is where most records of the Cathar settlement end. All that is known of them from that point on is that they retreated even further away from the river and took up a settlement on the far side of the pass that came to be known as Stony Lonesome. No one knows exactly why they moved. The area they moved to is hillier and not as fertile. It is farther from the river, which was the primary trade route used in that area at the time. In hindsight, the move makes no sense to any anthropologists who have studied that particular area.

No matter that we do not know why, the fact is that they moved. They abandoned their wood and timber houses and began the more arduous task of building houses out of stone. Not only were the houses built of stone, but a stone fence was built around the entire settlement. Walled stone walkways connected each building to its neighbor. In some cases, these walkways were even roofed over with stone so that the settlers could move from place to place without ever being out in the open. The handful of visitors that did pass that way and attempted to communicate with them described a community that had crossed over the line of sanity. No one would come out and greet them. Conversations were brief and barely lucid and were uttered through shuttered windows or gaps in walls.

It is amazing that a community such as this would last for more than a season but reports of contact with them continued for a year and a half. The final stories of contact were horrifying. Visitors described peering through chinks in the stone barriers and seeing pale, naked, filthy people with long unkempt hair. They looked like they had not been out in the sun for months and they seemed to have developed a permanent stoop from scuttling around in their squat, stone cells. At the end, they seemed incapable of, or at least unwilling to, communicating with outsiders.

Winter came that year, milder than most recent years. There was no reason that an entire community would have been unable to survive such a winter but when the snows began to melt and civilization continued to push its way out from the growing city at the tip of Manhattan Island, the first visitors at this stone asylum reported finding nothing. They did not report finding mass graves or abandoned homes filled with rotting remains. They found nothing. Further searches of the nearby area revealed the graves of only a few of the settlers and in one room

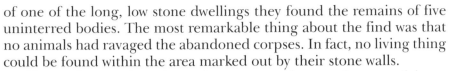

of one of the long, low stone dwellings they found the remains of five uninterred bodies. The most remarkable thing about the find was that no animals had ravaged the abandoned corpses. In fact, no living thing could be found within the area marked out by their stone walls.

No one knows where the settlers went or what ever became of them. No stories from the native tribes in the area reported any violent conflicts with settlers in the area. No tribes showed an influx of lighter skinned descendants from that time that would have indicated the settlers left and intermarried with the natives. No group or individual ever was seen in any of the surrounding villages or hamlets. No signs of any settlements that would have sustained such a large group have ever been discovered to show that they had moved yet again. They simply vanished. Based on estimates from ship's data and reports of visitors, approximately 130 people were never seen again.

That statement should actually be revised. They were never seen or heard of, *alive*, again. Visitors to the area today will often report hearing guttural whispers just over their shoulders, spoken in outdated Spanish. Many who have dared to investigate the ruins have reported feeling the brush of unwashed hair against their face and have felt a rancid foul breath on the back of their neck as if something was stooping over them, eager for them to leave. Or perhaps eager for them to remain forever. Archaeologists have even given some credence to these stories by refusing to excavate there any more. On more than one occasion, researchers have begun a study of the site to better understand who these people were and where they went. These studies have all ended tragically. Artifacts that have been taken from the site and placed in museums have often been removed from the exhibit and replaced with a tag that says "Artifact removed for refurbishing." Those artifacts have never been returned to their place in the exhibit. The "refurbishing" has often been a frantic journey back to the site of the village where the artifact has been hastily replaced within the stone labyrinth. The stories that accompany the reasoning behind the return of items taken from the site range from injuries to unemployment to bankruptcy and even to death. One tragic brush with fate after another seems to follow those that take from the site.

The most frightening aspect of this relic of a mission is the shadows that seem to adhere to people who stay too long in the environs. Many adventurous souls have spent the day exploring the area, searching for some bit of a memory of days past. A spoon, a window sash-weight, a lost coin, or merely a "feeling" of days gone by. Invariably though, if they stay past that time of day when the sun begins to set, they will cast more than a single shadow on their way out. A dark gray shadow has been reported to follow many that linger past dusk. It is as difficult to get rid of as it is to wipe rendered fat off of cloth. It is a grease stain on the soul that darkens those who do not bide the warnings of the more cautious.

Hunters and hikers in the area have on several occasions reported seeing large groups of people moving in and around the collapsed stone walls. Some of the witnesses have said that as they drew closer to investigate what all of these people were doing in the middle of the woods, the individuals who they were observing became fainter and fainter as the witnesses got nearer. By the time that they arrived at the site of the stone buildings, the people who they had been watching had faded away into shadows. Some have reported seeing these people involved in some sort of rituals while others have described the people that they have seen as doing nothing more than huddling in the corner of a stone building, gnawing on a bone. The numbers reported have varied from only one or two, to as many as over a hundred. At least a few of these reports have described the individuals seen as being completely naked, leaving several of them to suspect that they were some sort of cult engaged in some unclean religious rites. Perhaps they are right.

10
The Dark Pool

Not all tales of ghosts who met their mortal end in a watery grave take place in the river or the reservoir. There is a reason that West Point was one of the first university campuses to have a public pool, but has not had one since before the Great Depression. It is the same reason that puddles of water suddenly appear on the floors in Eisenhower Barracks and Pershing Barracks; the reason that the voices of small children are often heard in the halls when no children are present.

The Pershing Barracks and Eisenhower Barracks complexes. The eastern ends of these two barracks sit on the area where the old athletic building and the old pool once stood. It is these two barracks that bear the brunt of the savagery of the out-of-control ghost of the deceased training officer. It is also in these barracks where the laughter of the two young boys is most frequently heard.

Captain Thompson, a training officer assigned to West Point, was known for his tyrannical leadership style. Many people described his "training" as dictatorial and gratuitously repressive and humiliating. His cruel interactions with others was not limited to just the academy cadets. His family also suffered at his hands. His plain but pleasant young wife was often seen in town with a bruise on her eye or over her cheek. At times, days might go by where she would not be seen at all. His two boys, six and eight, were often seen to cower in his presence although he was never seen to hit them, at least not in public.

The two boys, however, loved being around the West Point cadets. Any fear of their father was overbalanced by their thrill of being allowed to associate with the young men of the academy. The feeling was mutual. The loathing that the cadets felt for Captain Thompson was more than matched by the love the cadets felt for the two young boys that followed them around like little two-legged puppy dogs. The two boys thought it the height of entertainment to walk behind the cadets in their formation and mimic their marching. When the command was given to "Right shoulder, arms," two tiny faux cadets in the near vicinity would shift imaginary rifles from one shoulder to the other. When "Present, Arms" was called out, the two diminutive, would-be soldiers would snap a more perfectly angled salute than half of the cadets in the corps. For their part, the cadets always managed to somehow get a hold of pieces of hard candy or sometimes even chocolate to reward the small recruits. It was not uncommon for the cadets to pass them used and worn pieces of gear or uniform either, so that in time, the two boys had complete, although slightly ragged and certainly oversized, uniforms with which to parade around in.

In the early summer of that year, Captain Thompson decided to teach his two young sons to swim. Now it must be understood that Captain Thompson, although a cruel and capricious man at times, loved his two boys very much and was tremendously proud of them. He simply was raising his children in a manner that he thought would be most beneficial to their development, misguided though it was.

His method of "teaching" them to swim was very similar to his other leadership techniques. Early in the morning, before most people were up, he took them to the pool. The pool at that time was located next to the gymnasium. (This area today holds parts of Pershing Barracks and Eisenhower Barracks.) He demonstrated to his boys the proper swimming technique. Then he promptly threw them in. They struggled, swallowed water, and sank. After a moment, Captain Thompson pulled them out of the water, allowed them to catch their breath, and then shoved them back in again. Over and over again he would let the boys get almost to the point of drowning before finally intervening and offering any assistance. Although some might consider this method odious, it did in fact work. Within a matter of weeks, the boys endurance and ability were rapidly increasing. It was a common sight all summer long to see Captain Thompson and his sons out at the pool before the sun was even up. By the end of the summer, the two young boys could swim as well as most of the cadets in the corps.

The tragedy occurred one morning near the end of the season. As the days got cooler, they also got shorter. This morning was particularly chilly and presaged the winter to come when the pool would no longer be an option. Most people would have considered this morning too cold for swimming lessons, but Captain Thompson was not most people. The changing season and shorter days meant that it was still dark when Captain Thompson and his boys arrived at the pool. This morning's focus was on survival swimming. Captain Thompson planned on making the boys tread water for the first thirty minutes and then swim laps for the remaining time. They were fifteen minutes into their treading water when the younger boy got a cramp. The child called out to his father requesting permission to come to the side of the pool and rest. He knew better than to simply take a break without permission. Captain Thompson of course, refused. He insisted that he had fifteen more minutes of treading water and that he should work the cramp out while he was treading water. The cramp became rapidly worse, however, and the little boy began begging for his father to let him come to the side. This only angered Captain Thompson even more and he started shouting at the boy, "Fifteen minutes! That is all I am asking. Stop your whining and give me fifteen more minutes!"

The boy began crying which made matters even worse. He went under water for a moment and came back up spluttering and coughing. His father angrily paced the darkness on the side of the pool shouting out, "Fifteen more minutes!" at him.

The boy went under again. This time he did not come back. Captain Thompson grew angrier at what he viewed as laziness and lack of effort. He shouted out even more vehemently at the spot in the dim water where the boy had disappeared. The younger boy still did not reappear. The older brother now, showing more sense than his father, realized that something was wrong. He started to call out to his father to help the younger boy. This only added to the shouting and the confusion. The father now redirected his anger at the older brother. Eventually though, something pierced his sense of outrage and he realized that the younger boy had been under too long. He had often let the boys go to the very brink of drowning in the past but this was too long. He looked everywhere across the surface of the gray shadowed water but saw no sign of the boy. Immediately, Captain Thompson dove into the water. He did not find the boy on the first dive, nor the second. It was not until his third trip to the bottom that he clasped something that was so still, he prayed that it was not his child's hand. As he struggled to pull the still form to the surface and then to the side of the pool, fear finally began to replace his anger.

He heaved the small, still body out of the pool and began pressing on the stomach in an effort to force out the water that seemed to have stolen the child's breath. Water slowly gurgled out of the blue lips but no intake of air followed. Captain Thompson pushed again and then slapped the boy's face, not out of anger but out of a desire to sting some spark of life into the pale face. There was no response.

He turned to the pool and called for the older boy to run to the barracks or to the hospital and get help. The pool was still. The older brother was not to be seen. The first light of dawn was filtering over the horizon and it turned the surface of the pool into a still, silver mirror; unbroken by any movement.

By this time, the shouting and the splashing had drawn a reaction from the cadets in the nearby division barracks. Several cadets arrived on the scene to find the body of the younger boy laying on the side of the pool and Captain Thompson continuing to dive into the pool in search of the older boy. Some of the cadets grabbed up the body of the young boy and attempted to minister first aid to the hopeless case while others dove straightway into the pool to help Captain Thompson with this search. It was only a moment before the body of the second boy was laid out on the edge of the pool alongside his brother.

There was nothing to be done. No amount of resuscitation, or pleading, or cursing would bring them back. Captain Thompson stared frantically at the two dead boys and then went coldly still. Those who were there said that a frightening transformation seemed to overtake Captain Thompson. They said that it was as if his very soul poured out of him and pooled on the ground along with the water that was still draining from his clothes. They said that it seemed that his eyes suddenly bulged out, or perhaps the skin retracted and pulled away from the sockets. He got a crazed look and suddenly stalked away and stormed into the nearby barracks.

A Storm of Fury

Those who were in the barracks and still unaware of what had happened said that he seemed like a man possessed. He began his most sadistic tirade ever. He stormed into rooms, searching out the most minor infractions and laughed gleefully when he was able to find an excuse to empty out the contents of a closet or dresser into an unceremonious pile on the floor. The rant got worse and worse. He turned over entire wardrobes and flipped beds with what cadets described as little more effort than knocking over a house of cards. And everywhere he went, he left streams of water, pouring off of his ruined uniform and puddling on the floor in neverending torrents.

His outrage soon turned from being directed at the inanimate furniture and clothing to being directed at the cadets themselves. He started to toss around cadets as if they were paper. One cadet was knocked unconscious when he was thrown almost twenty feet down a hallway. There was no telling how bad the abuse could have gotten had not one cadet had the sense to run and seek help from other officers. In the end, it took four adult officers and five cadets to restrain him.

In the end, Captain Thompson was taken to the hospital and heavily sedated. It was the only way to keep him calm. He had broken through a set of restraints and the decision was made that for the safety of the staff as well as his own safety, for now he would have to be completely unconscious.

As the base commander, the MPs, and the cadets sorted out the tragedy of the morning, it finally dawned on someone that Mrs. Thompson had yet to be informed about the tragic death of both of her sons and the apparent loss of sanity of her husband. No one wanted to be the messenger that delivered that message. In the end, it was a committee of three cadets who were particularly close to the boys who took on the task. They walked the mile from the barracks area out to the section of the base called Camp Town where many of the staff of the academy lived. With a mother's intuition, Mrs. Thompson surmised their message from the moment they appeared on her doorstep. She became overwrought but then settled down surprisingly quickly. The cadets offered to stay and help her with anything that needed to be done but she insisted that she was okay and asked them to leave. Mournfully, the cadets acceded to her wishes.

On a base the size of West Point, it was not long until everyone knew the story. Activities on the post seemed to go into slow motion throughout the remainder of the day. The final act, however, would not be played out until the following morning. When the shift change at the hospital occurred early that morning, Captain Thompson was found to be missing from his bed. The restraints were still in place and the night shift assured the morning shift that they had administered the proper sedative. A search was immediately initiated. It was their fear that in his manic state, he might injure or even kill someone.

Almost before it began, however, the search was called off. Captain Thompson had been found. An early morning cadet who happened to be passing by the pool, the site of the previous day's tragedy, saw a gray form floating in the gray pool. He immediately dove in. The body that he pulled out was that of Captain Thompson.

The post desperately wished to put this tragic episode behind them. Under pressure from the administration, the investigation quickly concluded that the Captain Thompson's death was a suicide, committed out of remorse for the accidental death of his two sons the day before. Later investigations, however, introduced other ideas regarding Captain Thompson's death. Mainly, that it might not have been self-inflicted or accidental and that it was possibly murder. The hospital staff testified that Captain Thompson had been restrained and sedated and could not have left the hospital without assistance. Additionally, there were many murmurings from the cadets themselves that no one was sad to see Captain Thompson gone and that if a cadet were responsible for the act, he deserved a reward. The possibility that a cadet (or even, cadets) snuck into the hospital, released Captain Thompson, and then murdered him certainly exists. He was hated even before the accident, and considering how much the cadets loved the two boys, it was certainly within the realm of possibility that one or more of them would have retaliated in this manner.

Another strong candidate for the murder, if murder it was, was Captain Thompson's wife. After suffering for years at his hands, would it be any wonder that the woman would have snapped and taken matters into her own hands when her abuser's actions caused the death of her only children? There was some credibility to this suspicion since Mrs. Thompson was never seen again at West Point. When an official party went to her house to inform her of her husband's death, they found the home empty. A suitcase was missing as well as most of Mrs. Thompson's personal effects. No sign of her was ever found again. No conductor on any nearby trains or passing carriages or motorists reported seeing a young woman that matched Mrs. Thompson's description. She'd simply vanished.

The incident was kept as quiet as any such tragedy can be kept. Nothing more than rumors ever made their way outside the walls of the academy. A search of the historical records of that time period reveal only this one entry: "CPT Seth Thompson, passed away due to accidental drowning, West Point, August 29th, 1911."

The Haunting

Since it was already late in the season and close to being closed anyway, the decision was made to close the pool immediately and not open it up until the following summer. That decision was unintentionally made permanent the next morning, however. Just before reveille the following morning, a loud crack awoke most of the cadets who lived in the barracks close by the pool. It was as loud as a cannon but had a distinctly different tone to it. Fearing yet another tragedy, dozens of cadets rushed to the pool. The ground around the pool was wet and marshy when they approached. When they got close enough, they saw why. The pool had split. Not a small discrete crack but a large gaping crevice that extended all the way across the floor and up the east side. The water was still pouring out of the hole even as they watched. Maintenance was called in to find the source of the hole but none was found. No reason was ever discovered for why the pool had suddenly split.

It was only a matter of days after this that strange incidents began to be reported around the barracks. Cadets began to report that someone had been in their rooms and had moved their things, in some cases, even violently thrown clothing and books around the room. One cadet even stated that he witnessed his heavy wooden bed being toppled over, narrowly missing him. Additionally, large puddles of water were found on the floor in the near vicinity of the incidents. A group of cadets who were in the hallways late one night even reported seeing a series of wet footprints appear, one step at a time, all the way down the hall.

Another common occurrence that began to plague the cadets at this time involved the clocks and watches. Timepieces all around the area were found to be set fifteen minutes off. At first, many instructors thought that this was simply an excuse that cadets were using to be late for class or to miss formation. In time, though, this was found to be a constant and invasive problem and some sought alternative explanations for these fifteen-minute lapses.

The final oddity that began shortly after this incident, was the sound of splashing and screaming that would emanate from the empty pool. More than once, would-be rescuers rushed to the side of the pool thinking that some poor soul was floundering in water that may have accumulated in the bottom, only to find the pool empty and deserted. One such incident so spooked the superintendent's wife that the decision was made that the pool would not be reopened in the summer and would instead be demolished. Even this did not stop the sounds. The filled-in earth would often issue forth horrible sounds of splashing and struggle and piteous cries for help from two young boys. The filled-in ground where the pool once stood would constantly ooze forth water.

About twenty years after the incident, the sounds that were heard in the area suddenly changed. Where before the splashing had been frantic and the cries had been pleading, now the sounds suddenly began to sound playful and the cries were cries of joy. Additionally, a third voice was now heard to echo ethereally next to the voices of the two boys. The voice of a young woman. For those who knew of the tragedy, it was assumed that somewhere the mother had passed away and had returned in death to where she had lost her boys. The sounds are now that of a happy family enjoying those moments of bliss that they had never been able to experience while the three of them were together and alive.

As for Captain Thompson, his voice is never heard lifted in laughter by the now-absent pool. This does not mean that he no longer visits West Point. On the contrary, even today, when cadets are late for class or their room is in a particularly horrible state of repair, it is said that Captain Thompson has been visiting them. This of course by many would be considered to be a joke. If only it were not for the puddles on the floor and the wet footprints.

11

The Dead Don't Always Stay Buried

When West Point was still a series of forts that extended from Redoubt Four to Fort Clinton at the edge of the river, and the nearest town with any official status was Cornwall, six miles further up the river, there was a need for a place to confine prisoners until they could be taken to the circuit court in Peekskill. The most logical place for a jail was on the military base, since they already had the impression of security there and a sense of formal authority. They also had the armed forces necessary in a period when an official sheriff was not a permanent position. That is how a civilian wound up being confined on the base. That is also how that same civilian wound up becoming one of the earliest spirits to haunt the halls of West Point.

In the early days of the base, the facilities were very spartan. In 1776, when the Revolutionary War had begun, there was little more than a lookout on the location. The Polish engineer, Thaddeus Kosciusko, began to build the first real defensive system at West Point the following year. Initially a dirt and wood structure that was later expanded into a five sided stone fort, the area along the eastern edge of the plain was originally called Fort Arnold. This fort was renamed Fort Clinton for obvious reasons following Arnold's attempt to turn traitor and sell the entire series of fortifications to the British. It was little more than a five-sided stone wall initially and covered only a small area. That fort was reinforced on the hill above with Fort Putnam, a stone-walled fort that was open on two sides, and then with a series of three small irregularly shaped forts on the hills above Lusk. These five "forts" were supported by artillery positions that provided some covering fire against anyone attempting to attack these first fortifications of West Point.

The administration building where the original cavalry barracks once stood. The cavalry barracks was the first building at this location. After the collapse, it was eventually replaced with a stable building. The stables were then renovated into the building that exists there today. You can still see the pulley assembly extending over the hay door on the second floor, directly over the main entrance.

As time passed, the space between these fortifications began to be filled in with additional construction. One of the earlier additions was a small cavalry barracks and a stable. This addition was housed on the hillside just above the area known today as Buffalo Soldier Field. This obviously was not the same barracks and stables that were built almost a hundred years later and have since been converted to serve as administrative offices, but it was in roughly the same location. This original building, however, is the reason behind why many of the administrative and identification services personnel serving in the newer buildings will not work after hours and never by themselves. Those employees know that the reason many of the photos at the ID shop turn out poorly or with strange images in the background has nothing to do with the photographic skills of the employees and everything to do with the restless spirit whose mortal remains still lie buried somewhere beneath the building.

A Muddy Issue

The problems with the photos at the ID center are probably the most well known of the incidents. It is often a joke with any type of government photos, (driver's licenses, school IDs, military IDs, etc.) that the pictures turn out notoriously bad. It is more than just bad pictures that plague the ID center at West Point. The pictures are often extremely unflattering or blurry. Annoying, but hardly disturbing. What really causes startled looks is when the face is in focus but the background looks muddy. Not blurry. Muddy. It looks as if the picture of the individual in the photo is superimposed over an image of a landslide. There is no sign of the nice clean wall that they use as their backdrop. No poorly focused image of a modern office in the background but a clear picture of a brown and black morass of slurry and dirt.

When the pictures were all analog and the photos had to be developed, it was usually written off by those who did not have to live with it every day as a chemical reaction that occurred during the processing of the negatives. When the center switched to digital right around the turn of the millennium, the problem was not corrected. Photo after photo would turn out just fine and then suddenly they would all start showing the muddy background again. No chemical developing was going on, so that could no longer be used as an excuse.

Even worse than the blurry photos or the muddy background, were the pictures in which other images were seen in the background. Strange half-formed faces staring, and sometimes, screaming, out of the muddy background. Again, before the digital change-over, these images were written off as badly formed double-exposures and faults with the film. The worst of these incidents happened right after the digital change-over when West Point got a new garrison commander. The new garrison commander showed up at the ID shop to have his official photo taken for the command wall. The first three photos had the familiar muddy background in place of the flags that they had posed behind him. The garrison commander was trying not to get irritated, but he had taken time out of his day to set up the appointment and it was hard to pretend that it did not irk him just a bit to have to do the photo over and over again. After the third photo it seemed that things were okay. The image the digital camera displayed on the computer seemed perfect. When they attempted to print it out, however, it appeared in the picture that the wall behind the garrison commander and the two flags was not the plastered wall of the office but was instead constructed of mud. And even more disturbing was the image of a face and the edge of a shoulder that seemed to be struggling to escape from the mud.

Now the garrison commander's irritation began to turn to anger when he started to suspect that someone was playing a practical joke on him. The camera operator assured him that it was nothing intentional. The operator of course knew what was going on but he hesitated to tell this new colonel for fear of how he would react. He simply asked the garrison commander to retake the photo and hoped that it would turn out right this time. It did not. The next photo was even worse as the mud-covered image seemed to lean even further out of the wall and a hand began to extend toward the garrison commander. In the photo after that, the mud encrusted hand was almost on the garrison commander's shoulder and the mouth on the muddy face was stretched wide, revealing startlingly white teeth against the bland brown of the mud.

The operator had no choice but to explain to the now furious garrison commander that this was a common occurrence. The garrison commander initially would not listen to the camera operator. After four more individuals from the office, all sober and normal individuals to all appearances, confirmed the story did the garrison commander begin to back down. It is not known whether or not he ever believed their tales but it is known that the picture that he provided for his command wall was taken at a photo shop in the nearby town of Peekskill.

Un-"Stable"

Odd photos are not the only strange occurrences in this building. By many accounts, they were the least of the problems. Consistent reports from all who have used these buildings, even back to their early use as stables, have reported strange activities. "Supernatural" is an adjective that is often used, as is "poltergeist" and the more generic, "haunted." Early stable hands would often report seeing objects, even the horses themselves, floating in the air. The buildings were closed for a while after the stables were shut down. Eventually they were transformed into office space. The activities continued.

One of the earliest reported incidents drew a connection back to the building's original use. In the 1960s, shortly after the renovations were complete and the offices were occupied, an employee who was working late reported seeing a horse walking down the hallway. He immediately ran to his office and called the MPs. The MPs responded, but by the time they arrived they found no traces of any horse. No tracks were found outside or inside the building. The first assumption was that some of the cadets had been playing a practical joke. A call was made to the stables, which had by this time been moved out to Morgan Farms. The stables were searched and no horses were reported missing. Everyone was quite certain that rebellious cadets had to be behind the horse appearance, but no one was ever able to find the cadet responsible, nor figure out how they got the horse into or out of the building without leaving any tracks or being discovered on the campus.

This was not the last time a horse was spotted in the buildings, both walking and floating. In addition to other objects levitating, chairs sliding across the floor, and muddy footprints appearing out of nowhere on dry, sunny days, there have been at least two documented cases where workers have reported seeing small blue fires appear in the air and a ghostly face moaning at them from the flames.

The most frightening manifestations of this particular spirit are those that happen to the individual themselves. Workers might be able to handle the strange sights and levitations if that was all that they had to endure. The sad truth of the matter is, however, that many employees have reported having sudden attacks of vertigo where they feel like the building itself is turning upside down on them. Sometimes these are so violent that it causes the person afflicted to fall down on the floor and even to vomit. And then there are the unexplained losses of breath. More than a few employees have been beset with the feeling that they cannot breath. They open their mouths but there simply is no air to draw in. A few employees have even passed out from this loss of breath and on occasion, this sudden lack of air has warranted an emergency call to the hospital. It is these last instances that most employees simply cannot endure and why they insist on always having someone working with them in the buildings.

So what is the source of these strange events? Why all these apparitions and activities at this one location? It goes back to the last time that the old building that originally stood on that site was used. The night that it rained and rained.

A Rainy Night

As was mentioned earlier, the area around Highland Falls lacked any sort of official government outside of what the Army base offered. On the rare occasion that someone in the area had to be held in confinement for legal reasons, there was a guard room attached to the stable and cavalry barracks that had a basement that served the purpose. The individual involved was simply locked into a spare store room and waited for transport or for the circuit judge to arrive.

Usually this resort was used for more serious cases, but one night in the early spring right before the turn of the seventeenth century, the individual who wound up in that spare room cell was nothing more than the town derelict. He was taken in for public intoxication, but was in no way even really considered a criminal. A sour man for sure, but an honest one. Bitter and cynical and with little left but meanness inside him, he might spit at you, but he was not the type who would wrong you. He had originally been a farmer, but as the fortunes of the day went, his farm had failed. He had taken on a job at a local mill, but the mill had closed. Most recently, he had taken to trapping, but the beaver population in the area had been greatly diminished by over hunting for the last hundred years. With little else left to do, he had recently taken to drinking. His once-pleasant demeanor faded more rapidly than did his dreams of ever becoming successful at anything.

During one of the nights that he had enough money to get deeper into his cups than usual, but not enough money to rent a place to stay for the night, it began to rain. The five or six streets in Highland Falls were becoming muddy channels of slow, brown water. The out-of-work, out-of-luck man had managed to slump down against the side of one of the buildings in town, his feet extending into the slow flow of the street.

A cavalry soldier who had been in town visiting a "friend," whose husband was away on business, saw the man slumped on the side of the road. Full of good cheer towards the world, the young cavalryman decided to help out the derelict. He had no money with which to help him, having spent it all on a new hat for his "friend," but he figured that at the very least he could give the man a dry night's rest. With much difficulty he hefted the mostly unconscious derelict onto his horse and rode with him back to the base.

Upon arriving at the cavalry barracks, he begged help from the corporal on guard at the time and together they managed to get the man off the horse, into the building, and down the stairs. They deposited him on an empty cot and left him to dry out, both figuratively and literally. Out of reflex, the corporal locked the door when they left.

Since there was no official arrest or reason for the man to be incarcerated, no report was filled out. The corporal went back to his table and the cavalier cavalryman went to bed. A few hours later the change of the guard occurred. The corporal was relieved by a private, the lower ranks usually drawing the worst of the shifts. The corporal was tired and bored and only made a brief mention of the derelict in the cell as he changed places with the incoming shift. The private then had little knowledge of who the man in the basement was or why he was there.

About an hour into his shift, the man in the basement awoke and began shouting. The private made his way down the stairs to see what the problem was. The derelict was disoriented and still mostly drunk and was demanding to know where he was and what was going on. The private, who had little patience, made no attempt to understand him, and after exchanging shouts with him for a few minutes, returned to his place upstairs. Since it was late and there was very little chance that anyone would be disturbing him the rest of the evening, the private began to indulge in a small bottle whose contents would have been very familiar to the man locked up in the basement.

By midnight, it had been raining for over fourteen hours straight. Any semblance of a polite spring rain had vanished hours ago and what was coming down now could only be described in apocalyptic terms, and likely with several references to an ark. Shortly after midnight, the derelict awoke again and started shouting. The private on watch, having already responded to the shouts once before and not being certain that he could have steadily maneuvered the steep stairs down to the basement safely, decided to ignore the yelling. If he had had full grasp of his faculties, he might have noticed something a bit different about the shouts that were filtering up to him from below, but as it was he saw no need to move from his safe and stable chair. It was not too much longer before the private had nodded off to sleep.

About two hours later, sometime around three or four in the morning, the shouting started again. It was difficult to hear over the roar of the flood that was pounding down upon the building from the sky but it was loud enough and frantic enough to wake the private from his slumber. Even in his hazy, fuzzy state, there was something about the shout that set the private on edge and made him sit up. He paused for a minute trying to orient himself and wipe the last remnants of sleep and whisky from his mind. The shouts continued and he struggled to hear what the man below was saying, but it was difficult to do with the booming roar of the falling rain pounding on the roof. He finally decided that he was going to have to get up and find out what was agitating the man so. He stood up from his chair and began moving toward the stairs. Suddenly, there was a loud rumbling sound and the building trembled under the private's feet. The private was startled at first, but then assumed that the rumble was nothing more than a lightning strike that had hit precariously close. Surprisingly, he could no longer hear the man shouting from below. The private turned his head and listened for any further sounds but there was nothing except the roar of the rain. Satisfied that the derelict had gone back to sleep, the private returned to his chair and returned to sleep.

Sunrise came but it brought no light. The black darkness became a reflective darkness as the sun found it impossible to pierce the curtain of rain. The private's replacement came on shift, but in the gloom of the day there was no mention made of the derelict in the basement below. The day shift passed. It was not until the corporal from the previous day came back on shift that evening that the matter of the man in the basement was brought up again. The corporal was surprised to find out that the sergeant on duty was not aware that there was someone below. That meant that the poor man had gone without food and water for twenty-four hours. It surprised both the corporal and the sergeant that the man had not called out to anyone asking to be fed or let out and they immediately rushed to the basement door to check on him. They opened the door to the basement stairs and were stunned at what they saw. The basement had ceased to exist.

Rescue

Two feet below them, down the steep narrow stairs, was a layer of mud and water. It seemed that sometime during the night, the constant and heavy rain had weakened the hillside into which the stable was built. The result was that an internal wall must have given way and the basement had become flooded with water and mud. It was impossible to tell if the entire basement were flooded or collapsed or just the area directly below the stairs. The two men immediately signaled the alarm bell outside the barracks, and in a very short time, the entire cavalry force, both enlisted and officers, were assembled and informed of the tragedy.

There was much debate as to how best to attempt a rescue. Some argued for digging in from the outside but the fear there was that the weakened hillside might collapse even more with any such efforts.

Eventually, the decision was made to attempt to dig out from the inside. They hoped that the building would provide some type of support for the attempt that would prevent a further slide and protect any rescuers or the prisoner himself, if he were still alive.

They dug for six hours. The results were depressing. Due to the confined space of the stairwell and the constant flow of water, no sooner would they dig out a space but the water and mud would flow back in and fill it up. They had only cleared an additional three feet of stairs and were still several feet away from reaching the floor of the basement. Their frustration increased when the mud suddenly shifted again. It completely covered the area that they had just excavated so that by three in the afternoon, they were right back where they had started.

Their luck seemed to change when someone was able to locate a pump to help keep the water out as they began to dig once again. The rain also started to let up finally. The initial excavation went quicker this time and they got to the point where now the problem was not the water but the oozing mud that kept trying to flow back in on them. They used planks and beams to try and shore up the digging area but this only served to slow things down even further by narrowing the area in which they were able to work. Slow as it was though, progress was being made.

Then they struck the rock. A large boulder had shifted with the mudslide and now completely blocked any more forward progress. Discussion ensued as to how best to attack this new obstacle. Suddenly, interrupting the debate was the sound of cracking timbers. The ominous sound precipitated an immediate rush up the stairs by those standing in the confined space in front of the boulder. One of the planks they had been using to hold back the mud suddenly shattered which led to the successive failure of all of their support beams. The persistent mud, with an almost personified malevolence, once again rushed back into their excavated space.

Everyone stood there staring at the space below the floor. No one spoke, but the communication between the men in the room was just as clear as if it had been a verbal debate. It was now after midnight. The collapse had occurred almost twenty-four hours previously. The derelict in the store room had likely been crushed by the initial mudslide. If not crushed by the mud, then he was likely drowned by the water that had surely filled up the space. And if not drowned or crushed, if by some miracle there had been a pocket of space left for him, he had almost surely run out of air by this time. In the best of circumstances there were still hours of excavation left ahead of them and no one had as yet come up with any solution as to how to move the giant boulder once they arrived at it again. Silently the rescuers began to trickle away until the only people left were the corporal, the captain of the troop, and the cavalryman whose good-will gesture had brought the man there in the first place. They held a sleepless and pointless vigil throughout the remainder of the night.

The rain ceased sometime during that dark night and the morning came bright and clear. The sun shone out as if it were trying to make up for the last two days. The volunteer rescuers all returned to the site to reassess the situation. Only in the clear light of day did the dire situation become fully apparent to all that stood in front of the building. The mudslide had not simply breached a basement wall but had completely collapsed the rear foundation wall and had shifted the entire building almost a foot off of its original foundation. The whole building was in imminent danger of collapse. The rescuers who had labored to save one life had unknowingly been putting themselves in serious danger simply by being in the building.

Demolition

The garrison engineers assessed the situation and determined that the building could not be salvaged. The decision was made to demolish the entire thing. That demolition never occurred. The building was simply left abandoned and over the next two years, time did the job for them. A second bout of torrential rain two years later finished what the earlier rain had started. The building collapsed. No attempt was ever made again to recover the body of the man who had been so unfortunately imprisoned in the basement.

That man, who was entombed in that mudslide over 200 years ago, still lies beneath the site today. His name is forgotten. His presence in the cell was forgotten after an intended act of kindness led to his passing away in a tortured and neglected manner. But now his restless soul haunts the building, determined that he will never be forgotten again.

An original photo of how the statue first looked upon its unveiling.

The grave of Custer in the West Point cemetery. The pedestal is still obviously the one that was used for the original statue but the statue itself is conspicuously missing.

12
The "Not Right" Statue

A n accusation often made by the cadets at West Point is that their tactical officers are too cold and rigid. Depending on who their tactical officer is, that is a claim that may or may not be true. There is one resident officer at West Point, however, for which the description "cold and rigid" is indisputably appropriate. George Armstrong Custer is best known for his tragic "last stand" at the battle of Little Bighorn, but perhaps that battle was not his last stand after all. Perhaps his last stand is still taking place on the campus at West Point and is the basis for the following tales.

Custer graduated from West Point in June of 1861, fifteen years before his ignominious death at the Battle of Little Bighorn. He graduated last in his class, but when the Civil War broke out only a few years later, every officer was needed, no matter what their ranking. Due to his audacious and aggressive maneuvers both on the battlefield and politically, Custer was soon granted the brevet, or temporary, rank of Major General. Following the war, he continued in the permanent rank of Lieutenant Colonel and moved out west to fight in the Indian Wars. In 1876, Custer was killed in the Battle of Little Bighorn. Initially he was buried on the site of the battle, but the following year his remains were moved to the cemetery at West Point. It is not, however, his ghostly presence that moves around the West Point campus today. It is, in fact, a much more tangible presence that has terrified many cadets at the Point.

After Custer's death, his wife, the daughter of a well-known judge, and some of Custer's politically connected allies, campaigned for a memorial to be erected to him at his alma mater, West Point. The initial plan that was introduced called for a small and simple stone memorial with a bronze plaque. That plan quickly morphed into a larger stone monument, then a monument with a bust of Custer, and then finally, a full-size statue of the man on top of a stone pedestal. The final plan was approved, artists were sought, and finally the statue was commissioned. Seven months later, the statue was ready.

Many people assembled at West Point for the unveiling of the statue. Friends, family, politicians, his widow, all stood by. Bands played, speeches were made, and finally, the sheet was removed.

Right away it was obvious there was something wrong. Everyone who had seen Custer personally commented on how remarkably accurate the image looked. It seemed as if the man had suddenly reappeared, cast in bronze. Those who knew him well, however, were put off by the statue. It seemed to many of them to be too life-like. Several people present spoke about being made uneasy by the statue.

The most dramatic reaction to the statue came from Custer's widow, Libby Custer. She immediately began muttering under her breath, "Not right, something's definitely not right about that thing." She could not even stay for the conclusion of the ceremony and simply walked away, continuing to mutter, "It's not right."

It must be understood that this was more than just odd. This was out of character for the widow, who was not only Custer's strongest advocate, but also depended on building and maintaining his legacy to keep her position and income. She wrote three books on the subject of her husband and went on countless speaking tours recounting what her life with the general, whose fame she was continuing to grow, was like. Libby never missed an opportunity to have a monument erected or a building renamed after her late husband, and yet almost as soon as the dedication of the statue at West Point was complete, she began calling for its removal. It couldn't have been due to the appearance of the statue itself because she had been intimately involved with picking out the artist and approving the pose and image. She knew better than anyone but the artist himself what the final product would look like, but something about it just put her off and made her uncomfortable. In the coming months, as she began to campaign to have the statue removed as vigorously as she had campaigned to have the statue erected, the only argument that she could allude to was that it was "not right."

Walking in West Point

The "not right-ness" of the statue began to manifest itself almost immediately. Only a few nights after the dedication, two cadets had snuck down to the area known as flirty walk to sneak a few drinks of smuggled alcohol. As the sun began to set, they started to make their way back to the barracks to make their next formation. The route back to the barracks took them past the site of the new statue. In their slightly fuzzy, but not drunk, state, they made it all the way past the site before they realized that something was "not right." They both turned around and stared at the pedestal trying to figure out what had struck them both as odd. Then it hit them. They were looking at an empty pedestal. The statue was gone.

Their first thought was that they had the wrong place. It was after all, very new. And it was starting to get dark. And they had been drinking. Maybe they just thought they were in the right place. They wandered back and forth, looking to their right and left, for several moments and even standing on the empty pedestal themselves before they realized that they were not mistaken and that the statue was indeed gone.

Their next assumption was that someone was playing a prank and had hidden the statue. That thought was obviously flawed though, since even in their confused state they realized that it would take a prohibitively large body of pranksters to move a two-ton statue. They then began to make the next logical assumption, the one that many other people would be making about them in the near future. That assumption was that perhaps they were "fuzzier" than they thought they were from the bootleg liquor and were seeing things. (Or not seeing things as the case may be.)

As they stood there staring at the empty pedestal and wondering where the statue had gone, they saw a gray figure approaching them through the dusk. Immediately, they thought it was one of their training officers and the problem of the statue paled in comparison to the realization that they had now likely missed their formation and were about to get in some serious trouble. They knew that by now they must have already been seen and running would only exacerbate the situation so they stood there waiting for the worst. As it turned out, they had no idea how "worst" it was really going to get.

As the figure got closer, they realized that it was not one of their officers. The image became more and more recognizable but their minds simply failed to process what they were seeing. The shock of what was slowly revealing itself to them combined with the rapid dissipation of the effects of the alcohol kept them from running until the figure was within only about ten feet of them and was clearly unmistakable. The image approaching them was none other than that of the missing statue, striding purposefully across the plain with its face set in bronze.

At about the ten-foot mark, their petrification vanished and they broke into a mad dash for the barracks. They came charging into the cadet area, out of breath and scarcely able to complete a coherent sentence. As they slowly got the details of their story out, their frightened appearance and the still lingering smell of alcohol led most people to believe, not incorrectly, that they had been drinking. Their passionate terror, however, was definitely a change of pace and many of the cadets rushed out onto the plain to see for themselves. Most of them had the intention of verifying that the statue was still indeed in place and using the whole incident to mock their two fellow cadets. Those intentions soon changed. As they crossed the plain, even at a distance, it was clearly evident that the statue was not missing and seemed to be exactly where it was supposed to be. When they got nearer, this was in fact the case. The statue was right where it was supposed to be. This did not enjoin criticisms of the two frightened cadets. Although there was absolutely nothing unnatural about its location or appearance, there was something menacing about the statue. Nothing that anyone could put a finger on, but simply something that was "not right."

The impromptu rush across the plain at that time of day, accompanied by the yelling of cadets and the angry shouts of officers ordering them back to their area, drew the attention of the superintendent who lived just across the plain from the activities. The image of the angry superintendent fast approaching them was something that would normally have frightened the cadets and the officers that had now caught up with them but the superintendent seemed mundane in comparison to that intangible unquiet that they were feeling. The superintendent felt it too as soon as he arrived. Instead of disciplining anyone for the noise or loss of decorum, he simply and quietly ordered everyone to go to their rooms, while glancing uneasily over his shoulder at the statue.

These stories of the statue coming to life and roaming the grounds began to grow in number and validity. It became one of the biggest boogeymen that the cadets talked about. On the positive side, incidents of cadets being out after hours dropped dramatically.

One of the most public and lengthy occurred when a cadet sergeant decided to drill his squad near the statue. He was one of those sorts of individuals that would have been a bully no matter where he had gone to school. The addition of a military uniform added no honor to his character, merely a more inflated sense of self-importance. He highly disliked one of the cadets in his squad. This cadet had the misfortune of the cadet sergeant finding out that he was very superstitious and deathly afraid of the Custer statue. The dark-hearted cadet sergeant thought that making his squad drill near the statue would be a great way for him to scare the cadet he disliked, which for him was a wonderful way to spend the afternoon.

The command "Fall in" is a command that is given in order to make the designated unit line up in even rows and lines in front of the individual giving the command. Sometimes the command is given to

"Fall in on the flag," which means that the unit is to line up facing the flag. Any person, location, or object can be the point of this command. In this instance, the squad leader gave the command to his squad to "Fall in on Custer." This of course meant that he wanted them to line up in rows and columns facing the statue of Custer.

The squad leader then took up a position directly behind the statue and began to shout out marching orders from his position on the statue's pedestal. He thought he was being quite clever by shouting out such commands as "Custer says, Left face, Custer says, About face." As simple people often are, he found himself greatly amused by these activities. The superstitious cadet only made matters worse by allowing himself to be rattled by the commands being issued from behind the statue. Drilling in such close proximity to the statue made him nervous and he started to make mistakes; facing left instead of facing right, turning the wrong direction on a march command and running into the person next to him.

This only delighted the cruel cadet sergeant even more and he began to deride the superstitious cadet by name and make fun of him. He began shouting out insults at the cadet in his version of a Custer voice. "What's the matter with you cadet? I was last in my class and even I could march better than you are."

The mocking cadet sergeant now came out from behind the statue so as to better see and direct his abuse of the nervous cadet. He positioned himself in front of the statue and took up a pose that was similar to the pose of the statue and continued his rant. He made the rest of the squad stand to the side while he focused solely on the poor cadet who was beyond help now and was simply getting more and more frustrated and confused. The cadet sergeant began intermingling commands to do push-ups with his marching commands. "Right face, cadet. Your other right. Do pushups, cadet. That's the problem with you cadets today. Too soft. That was part of my problem at Little Bighorn. Too many of you soft officers that didn't know how to handle yourselves. Sure, I didn't actually have a plan when I attacked the Indians, other than to keep my pretty, curly hair from getting all messed up, but…"

Suddenly all of the cadets in the squad, except mercifully the superstitious cadet who was face down on the ground doing push-ups, screamed. The heavy arm of the statue ripped itself from its place and swung around. The squad leader now, who had had his back to the statue, found his screams joining the rest as the stiff, bronze arm crashed into his side and sent him sprawling. The statue then stepped off of the pedestal and started slowly advancing on the prostrate cadet sergeant on the ground. The entire cadet formation scattered and started running for the barracks. The cadet sergeant was only just saved from being crushed underfoot, when the cadet that he had only seconds before been mocking, grabbed the injured cadet sergeant and helped him to his feet. The two stumbled across the plain with the statue lumbering after them like a bronze Frankenstein.

There was no way that this incident could be hushed up or explained away in any rational, believable sense. An entire squad of cadets had seen the statue leave its base and at least a dozen more had witnessed the figure lumbering, more rapidly than one would think stone could lumber they say, across the field. The squad leader had to be taken to the infirmary where he was treated for a broken arm and two cracked ribs. The official story was that he had been goofing around while directing drill and had fallen off the statue while climbing on it. Everyone at the Point knew the truth.

"Gone"

Even at this early point in time West Point had its share of tourists but after this incident, many of the tour guides began avoiding that area of the plain. Guests would ask about the location of the statue of the famous Indian War fighter, but all they would get is a mumbled excuse or at best, a wave toward a distant bronze figure that they would never go near. The few visitors who would wander over on their own to view the statue would all agree that there just seemed to be something "not right" about it. Meanwhile, Custer's widow was continuing her campaign to have the statue removed. The sentiment at the point began to be in keeping with Libby Custer.

The final straw came one evening when the superintendent and his wife were hosting out of town guests. The female guest who was staying with them suddenly let out a scream one evening. When the household came running to see what was wrong, the guest reported that she had seen a man all dressed in gray, staring in the window at her. When she described the man she had seen, there was no doubt in the superintendent's mind. What she had seen had been the statue of Custer.

The following day the superintendent submitted a plan to the academic board to have the statue removed. There was no excuse or reasoning given. Everyone knew the why. In an era that was often typified by drawn-out arguments between the superintendent and the academic board, the vote was uncharacteristically swift and unanimous.

The morning following the vote of the board, the residents of West Point woke up to find the statue of George Custer gone. No moving equipment had been seen. No pulleys or hoists or cranes had been constructed as had been the case when the statue had first been installed. Yet when the sun rose that morning, the pedestal was empty.

Officially, the administration of the academy simply said that the statue had been "moved." No explanation for how it was moved or where it was moved to was ever offered. Anyone who mattered knew the truth. The statue had somehow known that it was going to be moved. It had been looking through some window or listening at some door and had heard what its fate was to be and had simply chosen to leave preemptively. Custer's widow thanked the academy for removing the statue while the officials shrugged and scratched their heads. Everyone was simply thankful that it was finally gone and no one cared to much to push the issue of "how."

It quickly became apparent, however, that "moved" might not be the same thing as "gone." Reports started coming in almost immediately of groups of students seeing the statue back on its pedestal. One group coming back late from a meeting at one of their professor's houses, saw a figure standing on the pedestal across the field. When they drew close to the statue, they said that the figure was certainly that of the famous soldier and that as they got near, the statue turned its head to look at them. When they reported this to their fellow cadets, this precipitated a mad rush back out on to the plain to verify the story. The group who had reported the new appearance trailed reluctantly behind the other cadets and were greatly surprised to find that the pedestal was once again empty. The following morning, a group of cadets who were out for an early morning run with one of the training officers, ran around the edge of the plain and also saw the statue back in its place. They too reported that as they drew abreast of the statue, the statue turned its head to watch them pass. (It is reported, perhaps apocryphally, that this particular group completed their run in record time.)

Whereas before the problem had been the statue leaving its pedestal, it now seemed that it was not going to be possible to keep him off of it. The superintendent attempted to organize an "ambush moving team" with all of the necessary moving equipment so that the next time the statue was spotted, they could move out immediately and corral the thing and move it for good, or maybe even destroy it. They were never able to utilize it though. The statue was simply too unpredictable.

Finally, the superintendent and the board, in another rare act of agreement, decided that something must be done with the pedestal. Although large enough to be a monument in its own right, it just seemed empty without the statue and drew too many questions from visitors and new cadets. Not to mention the issue of the haunted statue. One suggestion was made to toss the pedestal into the Hudson River so that if the statue of Custer returned, it might find itself mired in the unforgiving mud of the river bottom. Eventually, however, the decision was made to move the pedestal to Custer's grave in the West Point cemetery. Officially, this allowed the pedestal to still serve as a monument to Custer. Unofficially, the hope was that the statue might finally find rest among the other ghostly residents.

This was not to be the case. It was not long after the move was completed before guests and tourists to the Point began to comment on the unsettling statue that sat atop the grave of Custer. It seemed that the statue still returned to its pedestal regardless of its location. The suggestion was once again made to cast the offending pedestal into the river, but the West Point bureaucracy found a solution that they thought might allow them to salvage at least something from their "monumental" fiasco. They decided to emplace a large obelisk on top of the vacant pedestal. This still allowed them their need to celebrate one of their own while at the same time removing the pedestal as a place to which the statue could return.

This solution seemed to work for a time. No more sightings were heard of for two years. The superintendent transferred out, secure in the belief that he had solved the problem. A new superintendent arrived and a new class of plebes were received. Then one morning, one of the new plebes looked out the window of the barracks and saw a still, gray figure standing in the courtyard, staring up at the barracks. This so unsettled the new cadet that he went running for his cadet lieutenant. The commotion brought many cadets to the window. Several staring faces looked out on an empty courtyard. The new cadets thought it was all a joke at first but the juniors and seniors who had been around for a while, knew that Custer was back.

The Haunting

Since that incident the statue has been seen many more places and many more times. Guests visiting the West Point cemetery still often comment on the lifelike statue that adorns Custer's grave. Only after the fact do they become uneasy when they are informed that there is no such statue at the site. A few of those brave souls have returned to the grave to see for themselves and wind up muttering that they knew that there was something "not right" about the statue when they had seen it. It has been seen many times near the original location where it was first placed. It has been seen in the cadet areas. Sometimes it has been seen on the bluff, staring out over the river. Once it was even reported in the middle of Michie Stadium. Sometimes it is reported as still, as a statue should be, while at other times it is seen to be moving.

One of the more disturbing stories involving a sighting of the statue occurred as the cadets were moving up the hill from the barracks to the cadet chapel. A small meditation garden exists on the hill below the chapel. The stairs that the cadets take up to the chapel pass this garden at a distance of no more than thirty feet.

As the cadets filed up the hill, someone noticed a figure sitting on the stone bench in the garden. Immediately, it became apparent that this figure was not a person. The visage of the figure was worn and tarnished, stained with verdigris. Not a hint of shine peeked from beneath the streaks of greenish gray. Those who had seen the figure before recognized it instantly as that of the statue of Custer. Many of the cadets took off running, as the statue was known to sometimes chase cadets and had injured unwitting cadets on a few occasions, but a few cadets noticed something different about the statue this time, not the least of which was the fact that no one had ever reported seeing it sit before. They stared as if mesmerized. Not only was the statue sitting, but it seemed slumped over, if metal can ever slump, and its face was being held in its heavy stone hands. Bronze curls of hair hung down almost covering the face. As the cadets stopped and stared, the figure raised its head from its hands and turned toward them. The cadets that saw the face reported that the statue looked sad and not its normal unsettling self and that there were dark lines down the side of the statue's face as if it were wet. As if it were crying. The statue then turned away again and put its face back in its hands. The cadets rushed off to find their training officer to report the incident. Several officers, the cadets, and the minister from the chapel descended back down to the garden but when they arrived, the statue was gone.

The statue is still seen around the academy even to this day. Sometimes moving, sometimes standing still. Sometimes menacing, sometimes simply observing. But always, something about it is "not right."

13
The Phantom Stage

In the hills above Merritt Road and behind Delafield Pond, there lies the remnants of an old stage road that once connected New York to Albany. It was first used back in the mid 1600s, but was the less desirable choice of passage since it was so hilly and wooded. Most people making the journey chose the slightly longer but easier journey through the area that is now Middletown. After the founding of the forts in the West Point area, the rougher route became more popular. The forts gave a sense of added protection since troops could ride out in either direction and react to emergencies if needed. The forts also created a draw for increased settlements and these settlements provided much support for travelers.

The stage road reached its zenith of use during the period between the 1780s and the 1850s. The series of forts at West Point grew and became one large base that then became the home for the United States Military Academy. The stage road ran right through the center of the fort and was used by civilians and military alike. For almost seventy years, it became the primary route of travel between the two major cities.

With the completion of the eastern rail line to Albany in the 1850s and the western line in the 1860s, the use of the route quickly began to decline. The last mail route was run on the road in 1881. It was still in use for a time after that, but its days were numbered. After commercial traffic eventually ceased, the military still continued to use the road. Eventually, it became so segmented with new highways being built that only portions of it were trafficable. It finally ceased to be used by the military in 1925. Publicly, the reason that the road was closed was for safety and so that the New Brick area of Camp Town (the derisive name for the housing area in which mostly enlisted people lived that served on West Point) could be expanded into a more family-friendly residential area. That is the story that the academy tells to explain the closure. Perhaps that is because the real reason would generate the wrong kind of publicity and it would hardly be acceptable for a modern university to admit that a ghost, or more properly, ghosts, had dictated school policy.

The real story began near the end of the decline of the road's use for commercial traffic. In the late 1870s, the road was still being used, but much more sparingly as had been done previously. The train was faster, more comfortable, and almost as inexpensive. The primary use of the road had dwindled to mail coaches and business of a military or government nature. It also acted as a nexus for travel that was of a more local sort, since West Point was the only train stop between Newburgh and Stony Point when it first opened.

The road as seen from just above the point at which the stage plummeted to its doom.

Of consequential note at this time was a minor silver rush that occurred in the Hudson Highland area in the late 1870s. Although nothing like the rushes in California, Colorado, the Dakotas, or even the Georgia gold rush of 1828, the Hudson silver rush of 1878-1879 was locally significant. The Highland Assays Office opened up on the post at West Point and miners from all around the Highlands would bring their ore into the office to be assayed. Only one or two mines actually turned any impressive profit, but it was enough to keep a couple of clerks employed in the two-room office next to the U. S. Post Office on West Point. There was even a small amount of gold that was panned out of Popolopen Creek that passed through that office. The source of the veins that provided the spare panfuls of nuggets from Popolopen was often sought but was never located.

Every few days or so, miners, local farmers, and even a few soldiers from the fort would bring in small sacks of ore or nuggets that would be assayed, weighed, and paid out. These sacks would then be stored in a room behind the office. The security in the office was minimal. The hope was that the implied security that the fort offered would be enough to deter any would-be robbers. Every two weeks these bags and sacks would go onto a coach that would pass through the fort on its way up to Albany. This might not have seemed like the best way to transport large amounts of valuables, since there was a train station just down the hill from the assay office. The truth of the matter was, however, that Highlands Assay was involved in a heated land dispute at the time with the much larger Hudson-Illinois Railroad Company that operated the trains that ran through the West Point station. It seems that the railroad claimed to own an easement on property that held a promising claim that the Highlands Assay had reportedly purchased from a down-on-his-luck (and quite possibly inebriated) miner. Because of this dispute, Highlands Assay had to transport all of its ore by the stage that was rapidly becoming outdated.

The Would-Be Outlaw

Into this scenario came Robert Atchison. Atchison was a local ne'er do well and itinerant thief who would have been thrilled had anyone ever referred to him as an "outlaw." By all accounts he was quite an intelligent man and very capable when he actually put his mind to something and followed through, but he was abysmally lazy and absentminded. He loved the *dime novels* of the Wild West and the badlands and thought of himself as a bit of a gunslinger. (Perhaps by the standards of the small population of Highland Falls, he was, but he was certainly no Bat Masterson.) He would dream of heading "out west" and "doing something," but these dreams never seemed to materialize. Inevitably, he would get bored or would fail to take any action beyond day-dreaming. He might work for a while as a farmhand or on the ferry runs, but then dreams of glory would draw him away to more unfulfilled unemployment. These bouts of unemployment would usually end up with a short-on-cash Atchison hatching some grand scheme that would amount to little more than a few tomatoes being stolen from someone's garden, or on an ambitious night, maybe even a chicken. Many of his larcenous acts were nothing more than stealing a new *dime novel* out of the general store or from someone's saddle bag when they weren't looking.

Atchison was destined for an ignominious and early death until fate intervened and guaranteed only the early part. Atchison's sister had married a man named Leonard Phillips. Phillips worked as a hostler at the stables on West Point. He was not an incredibly bright man and was easily awed by Atchison's tales of what great deeds he was going to do someday. Much to Atchison's sister's chagrin, Phillips would often invite the out-of-work Atchison over to their small home to eat dinner and regale them with tales of his "someday" plans. On one of these occasions, Leonard began telling Atchison about the stage that came through the post and picked up the silver and gold. He had heard during one of the last runs that some of the guards that accompanied the stage would often frequent a brothel just up the road in Cornwall. Because the stage was viewed as safe while it was on the Army post, the guards would usually ride ahead to Cornwall as soon as the stage made it to the assay office. The guards would then just fall in with the stage once it made it to Cornwall. This gave them extra time at the brothel and only left the stage with minimal guard for the three miles between the post and Cornwall.

Leonard Phillips' off-handed comments would soon determine the lives of fifteen men. It did not take much for the ambitious Atchison to formulate a plan. He was going to rob a stage coach, just like the outlaws in the *dime novels*. Initially, he thought that he would hit the stage somewhere between West Point and Cornwall. The more he thought about it though, the more he figured that the closer he hit the stage to the Army base, the more relaxed the guards would be and easier to take by surprise. As the plan took shape, however, Atchison's arrogance got the better of him. He decided that he could do better than just an ordinary outlaw who robbed a stage. He was going to pull off the most audacious robbery of his time and increase his odds of success at the same time. If the guards were going to be relaxed and easy to hit when they were near the post, they would be even easier to hit when they were actually on the post. He was going to rob a stage on a military base.

The plan was to recruit six men who were good shots with a rifle. Usually, there were five guards for the stage. If only two of them went on ahead to the brothel, that would leave three guards. One would be on horseback, and the other two would either be inside the stage itself, or possibly on the buckboard with the driver. Atchison figured that if two riflemen targeted each of the guards, they were bound to take them down and stop the stage quickly, even if one of the riflemen missed. Then a rush at the stage and a couple of quick shots would finish off anyone still alive inside and the stage would be theirs.

If the stage was going to be hit on post, there was really only one place to do it. The road that the stage always took began down by the north dock and wound its way up the hill, past the ordnance compound where the assay office was located, past the northern most tip of the plain, around the Catholic chapel, and then up into the hills behind the residential area of Camp Town, before hooking back into the Cornwall road. The hilly area was the only part of the road that was isolated enough to infiltrate and was perfect for an ambush.

Atchison began recruiting his gang. Leonard Phillips was the first dupe to be inducted into the motley crew, followed by Cameron McIntye, who held down a job as the town lush, Phillips' neighbors, the two Downing brothers who were down-on-their-luck farmers, and two other men whose names have been lost to record. None of these men were the crack marksmen that Atchison had wanted, but crack marksmen don't always advertise their stage robbing skills and he was too lazy to put much effort into the search.

The area was easy enough to scout out. There was little in the way of security around the remote edges of the post. The area was heavily wooded and hilly so there were no houses around. The position that he chose as his ambush was at a point where a bend in the road was bounded on one side by steep hills and the other side by a ten-foot drop down the road's retaining wall and then another fifty feet of steep downhill. The stage would be traveling slowly at that point and the guards would be out in front of the stage or behind it on the narrow road, making them easier targets than if they were riding out away from the stage.

The morning of the attack came. Atchison and his six-man crew met up at the Monroe-Cornwall intersection and stashed their horses back in the tree line. It was only with minor difficulty that they made their way in the pre-dawn darkness through the woods to the hill above the ambush site. Most of their problems came from Cameron McIntye, who had already been working hard at his job since the night before and barely managed to keep from shooting his drunk head off. Atchison positioned his band in groups of two along the high side of the road. He gave each group strict instructions to target the same individual so that it would be certain that at least one of their shots would take him down. Atchison then positioned himself in a spot closer to the road. He had visions of novel illustrators drawing him bravely charging the disabled stage with his pistol drawn to deliver the coup de grace through the stage door. They all settled in to wait.

First light appeared and not too long afterwards, the first sounds of the stage rolling up the hill could be heard. Then a glimpse of it was seen as it rolled around a far corner. Soon it would be within range. As the stage came down the road and approached the large white boulder that Atchison had designated as the trigger point, it seemed luck was on their side. There were no guards on horseback. Only the guard on the buckboard, and the two guards inside the stage, who could clearly be seen through the large open windows. Almost perfectly according to plan, the stage rolled up to the boulder and six shots rang out.

It was at this point that a glaringly obvious flaw in Atchison's plan revealed itself. Although Atchison had given strict instructions for each pair of gunmen to target a single man, he had not specified which man each group was to target. By a strange act of fate, all six gunmen fired at the one guard that was riding on the seat next to the driver. The result was that the guard on the buckboard went down immediately with three bullets piercing him. The driver also went down when one of the rounds meant for the guard missed and grazed his temple, knocking him from the stage but leaving him very much alive. No one had attempted to target the two most well-defended and covered men inside the carriage.

To make matters worse, other flaws in the plan were quickly revealing themselves. Like the fact that Atchison had assumed that a stage with no drivers would simply stop. He had not taken into account how a stage with no driver and two spooked horses might react. The two startled horses bolted. They accelerated into the turn that they had been slowly negotiating. The back of the stage swung over the edge of the stone retaining wall. Horses and stage started rapidly sliding backwards. Just as it looked as if the stage would pull the horses over the edge, the horses' traces snapped. The stage immediately dropped out of sight while the frightened horses continued running on down the road, trailing bits of reins and yokes behind them.

The stage had been somewhat slowed in its fall by the efforts of the horses. It plummeted another twenty feet down the hillside but had been slowed enough that it was stopped by two trees before it could go any further. One of the guards survived the fall with only a few scratches. The second guard was not so lucky. The tumult as the stage tumbled down the hill had quickly snapped his neck. He was dead even before the stage came to a halt.

Atchison immediately jumped out of his hiding place, followed quickly by the rest of his gang, with the intent of rushing the stage and finishing off anyone who was alive inside. They were quite surprised when the second interior guard popped up out of the upturned stage and began firing at them. He got lucky with his first shot and the slow brother-in-law, Leonard Phillips, was the first of the bandits to go down. The rest of the gang took cover along the edge of the road. Atchison finally began to show some quick thinking and leadership ability when he ordered three of the gang to pin the guard down while he and another member snuck around the side to try and get a clear shot at the sentry.

Time, however, was now against them. They had initially planned on conducting the whole operation with a single volley and perhaps one or two single shots to follow up. Near a military post, it might be enough to make people aware of it, but it was not likely to draw unwanted, extended attention. They would have time to make their escape before anyone was even aware something was wrong. Now it was different. They were involved in a drawn-out gunfight and it sounded like it. Shots were rapidly being exchanged back and forth from both sides and it was only a matter of time before someone came to investigate. Their escape time was rapidly dwindling.

The guard was not able to get any more well-aimed shots off. Every time he dared to raise his head, a volley of shots quickly drove him back inside the stage. He was reduced to trying to fire his rifle blindly over the side of the upturned stage. Atchison and his partner were able to flank the guard who realized what was happening too late. They came in on the side and fired several rounds directly in through the back window, silencing the guard forever.

They were now far behind schedule. One of their partners was dead, the stage was perched precariously twenty feet down the hill, and the extended gunplay had almost certainly alerted someone. They quickly scrambled to locate the boxes of silver and gold and get away while they could. At this point, they discovered the only piece of good luck that would occur to them all day. One of the more reclusive miners had not been to the assay office in over a month, most likely due to the heavy rains. That miner just happened to have had his best month ever. And it was gold ore that he had brought in. Not silver, but high-grade gold ore with veins so thick that you could have almost scooped the soft metal out of the rock with a pocket knife.

This piece of good luck, however, quickly became their undoing. The sight of the soft yellow metal drove the men practically insane with gold lust. The ore took up two more boxes than they had originally planned on carrying. A reasonable man would have determined that with one man down they would just simply have to leave at least one of the boxes behind, but they were determined to get it all. Like stubborn children, they began lugging the boxes out of the stage and up the hill.

Their bad luck did not get any better. The guard mount from the main garrison was much quicker than they had anticipated. The first

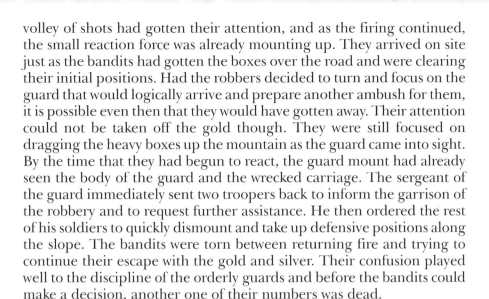

volley of shots had gotten their attention, and as the firing continued, the small reaction force was already mounting up. They arrived on site just as the bandits had gotten the boxes over the road and were clearing their initial positions. Had the robbers decided to turn and focus on the guard that would logically arrive and prepare another ambush for them, it is possible even then that they would have gotten away. Their attention could not be taken off the gold though. They were still focused on dragging the heavy boxes up the mountain as the guard came into sight. By the time that they had begun to react, the guard mount had already seen the body of the guard and the wrecked carriage. The sergeant of the guard immediately sent two troopers back to inform the garrison of the robbery and to request further assistance. He then ordered the rest of his soldiers to quickly dismount and take up defensive positions along the slope. The bandits were torn between returning fire and trying to continue their escape with the gold and silver. Their confusion played well to the discipline of the orderly guards and before the bandits could make a decision, another one of their numbers was dead.

This left Atchison with only four remaining members. He tried once again to quickly organize them. He placed two of them on commanding positions on the hill above the road. The rifles of the two dead men and extra ammo were given to them and they were told to hold off the guard as long as they could. Atchison knew now that there was no way that they could get the heavy boxes back through the mile of woods to where the horses waited. He decided that the only chance to get away and still keep the treasure was to find someplace on the rocky hillside to stash the loot. They would hide the treasure, escape, and then come back for it after the search was over. He and the other two members began trudging up the hill, dragging the boxes behind them, searching for a place to hide it.

The two bandits left on rear guard duty were actually very efficient. The reserves from the main garrison began arriving but because of the commanding position that they held and the generally steep and rocky nature of the hillside, the soldiers were unable to unseat them from their position. Lieutenant Pyle was content to simply wait them out. He was intelligent and patient and saw no need to risk lives in a quick assault on the position. He settled into a siege mentality. A second group of reinforcements arrived and Pyle sent them to patrol the road out to the Cornwall junction with orders to find and fix the bandits. No charges, no attacks. Simply locate them and pin them down. Eventually he knew that time and numbers would win the day for him. When the third squad of reinforcements arrived, he took them around the southern side of the hill on a more difficult route to cut off the remaining route to the Monroe-Cornwall junction. He now was quite certain that he had the bandits sealed up in the triangular area that was centered on the rocky peak overlooking the road.

Throughout the rest of the morning he continually road back and forth and sent messages by couriers to keep track of the lines. Atchison was reportedly seen by the picket along the Cornwall road somewhere around mid-morning but as ordered they did not pursue. They merely attempted to halt him with a few shots. By noon, Pyle began advancing the lines along the mile long flanks, keeping the two bandits along the road pinned down the entire time. As the afternoon wore on, one of the soldiers along the Cornwall line was felled by a shot from the upper elevations. The natural impulse to rush in for revenge was held in check and the line continued its advance, more deliberately this time and working from cover as they moved. They came upon a lone bandit that had taken a position similar to the one that the two bandits on the road had taken. It was not as well concealed, however, and there was only one of them so it was difficult to cover himself from multiple directions, but still, they did not attack. They simply fixed the position and did not let him do more than fire off poorly aimed shots for the rest of the day.

As night time drew near, the decision was made to hold the positions until the morning. The two bandits at the original ambush site had not had any food all day and had no more than a canteen of water between the two of them. The lone bandit fixed on the Cornwall side of the hill was likely in the same position. Only Atchison and one unknown bandit were still moving about in an area that had now shrunk to less than a third of a mile around the peak. The numbers of soldiers had swollen to well over 150, and were supplemented by several platoons of cadets who were anxious for action. They waited for morning.

As morning broke, LT Pyle was at the original ambush site. He called out to the two bandits to show themselves and surrender. It was at that point that Cameron McIntye rose from his position and charged the soldiers. Apparently, he had had more than water in his canteen. He had decided to quit the banditing business and go back to his more stable, although less ambitious job, as the town drunk. Unfortunately, he failed to convey this to the soldiers surrounding him. He also failed to put down his rifle as he came down the hill. The end result was that Cameron was soon relieved of all positions, at least in this life. After much more calling out to the remaining bandit overlooking the site, the advance and flanking began. After thirty minutes, the soldiers overran the site only to discover that one of the shots from the previous day must have found its mark. The remaining robber had apparently died sometime the previous day and was now cold and stiff.

The lone bandit in the position on the opposite side of the hill was much more fortunate. Using clear communication he was able to successfully surrender. That left only Atchison and one more man somewhere on the peak in an ever narrowing area of retreat. By mid-morning of that second day, the lines had closed in until suddenly more shots rang out. Another soldier, this time one of the cadets, fell, mortally wounded. Atchison had been found.

The position that he held was probably the strongest position so far, but the area was simply too small and the numbers were too overwhelming. The end was predictable. Atchison's plan for outlaw glory had flown and he could not live with the embarrassment of failure. Atchison's lone partner went down fighting and Atchison himself continued to shoot whenever he had a target. The soldiers were left with no option but to storm the position. When the final assault ensued, Atchison was struck by five bullets and was killed almost instantly. The soldiers who searched the site discovered that he had been down to his last four rounds of ammo.

What the soldiers did not discover were all the boxes of gold. Although two of the five boxes were found at the initial ambush site, the three boxes that Atchison took up the hill with him were not found. There was no evidence of an unknown partner that might have escaped with the treasure. Interviews with the lone surviving gang member confirmed that all bandits had been accounted for and it would have taken at least three men to drag the boxes out of the woods. It seemed that an extensive search would certainly turn up the missing boxes. The bandits had had no intention of burying or hiding the loot initially, so they had brought no implements that would have assisted them in hiding the ore well. Wherever it was, it had to be somewhere that two men could have placed it in a twenty-four hour period with minimal tools. This meant that it was buried in a shallow hole somewhere on the hillside or perhaps stashed in a ready-made cache location in one of the many small caves that dotted the hillside. Perhaps the boxes had been stowed in a crevice and had been covered with rocks to camouflage the site. Either way, the treasure was never recovered. The lone bandit survivor was sent to Fort Leavenworth since the crime had been committed on a military installation. He was released after seventeen years but never returned to New York.

A Robbery Repeated

It was not until after this bloody loss of eleven souls that strange events began to occur along that section of road. The very next stage that went down the road two days later, came roaring back down the hill at a dangerous pace. They reported to the guard mount that they had seen a stage being robbed and had watched the stage plummet over the edge of the road. Lieutenant Pyle, who was still the commander of the guard, immediately responded with nervous echoes of the previous events ringing in his head. The guard log of 27 August of that year is as follows:

0810 – Charlie Chambers [stage driver for the West Hudson Line] reports stage robbery, western slope of Camp Town hill, on Cornwall Road, guard dispatched.

0847 – Guard returns with no report of stage between garrison and Cornwall junction, Lieutenant Pyle and guard ride out with Charlie Chambers.

No further entry regarding the incident was found in the log. A letter from Lieutenant Pyle to his father was much more revealing.

Greetings to you father, from your son, serving faithfully at the military academy garrison,

I hesitate to relate to you the strange events of this morning lest you think me flitty or having taken up alcohol as your fear has oft been voiced to me in the past but be assured that I am sober and sound of mine when I write this to you. I do not purport to understand these events but relay them to you in their entirety, seeking your wisdom and counsel as to how best to perceive them.

You do recall that only last week, a heinous robbery attempt took place upon our base. It was then, with great alarm, that once again this morning I received a report of a stage being robbed. Immediately dispatching the ready mount, I prepared the reaction force to ride out if need. No stage had left garrison yet this morning, I must point out, and none were scheduled to arrive. Additionally no shots had been heard, as was contrary to last week's event. Not wishing to overreact, and waiting a signal from my sergeant, I held the reaction force at the ready until such signal arrived. Just over half of an hour had passed when the guard returned. They reported no such event as Mr. Chambers had reported and no sign that any carriage had yet passed that way.

Immediately questioning Mr. Chambers and examining him for signs of alcohol, against which you constantly warn me, and upon his oath that he had indeed seen a robbery occur, I placed Mr. Chambers upon a horse and directed him take us to the site.

With some amazement I rode with Mr. Chambers to the very point at which last week's robbery had transpired. With no show of loss of calm, and you would have been proud of me sir, I listened as he relayed a story that was lacking in only one detail from that event which I did relate to you but days ago. Namely, he did tell us, step from step, what had transpired from the first shot of the bandits to the plunge of the carriage over the side. With amazement I watched him walk in those very steps that the actors themselves had trod. The only detail that was absent from his account was that upon recalling the incident, Mr. Chambers stated that he saw everything happen but could not recall a single sound. He saw shots fired but heard no report. He saw horses bolting but heard no hooves or whinnying. He saw a stage go over the side of the road but heard no wood splintering or trees breaking.

Certainly, sir, the two questions that occurred to me have already occurred to you. First, that the man was drinking and had been a victim of a flight of fancy, brought on by that demon you constantly preach against. I can assure you sir, that Mr. Chambers is a strong Quaker man and was not at the time nor ever has been known to touch alcohol, or what you refer to as "that infernal spirit." Second, that the man fabricated the story for some reason of folly. This is also not in keeping with his character and ever were he wont to do so, he would not have had such intimate knowledge of the crime. The men of course, then being of a superstitious mind, began the inevitable discussion of spirits and lost souls of those recently departed.

I can see no reason of this and so ask of you your advice and thoughts on this matter. I will respectfully await your reply.

Your obedient and sober son,
Daniel P. Pyle

No further comments of reports regarding this particular event are known to exist. Over the course of the next eight months, however, no fewer than twenty-two reports of the phantom stage robbery were reported to the guard and resulted in deployments of troops. Three of the reports were written off as alcohol related, three more were concluded to be pranks. That left sixteen reports that had no natural explanations. And every report was the same. A silent pantomime of the robbery occurring over and over again, in the exact same location, with exact same events replaying themselves.

The reports became so frequent, and so disruptive, that the road was simply disused. Stage drivers began taking their coaches over the slightly steeper and more difficult pass that would eventually become highway 9W. Still the reports continued by those rare, infrequent souls who chose to bravely or ignorantly pass that way. A robbery playing itself out in total silence, over and over again. All commercial traffic on that section of road finally ceased in 1897 when the post boundaries were surveyed and more clearly defined and no more through traffic was allowed.

The silent apparition continued, however. Diminished in number certainly, but that was only to be expected due to the decrease in traffic. That section of road was still usable well into the twentieth century and was utilized to get to and from different training areas by military personnel. It was common to hear about cadets going on an exercise and reporting that as they rounded the bend in the road on their horses, and eventually, in their jeeps, to report the mimed attack and silent deaths. The Army steadfastly refused to acknowledge the apparitions even though over 200 pages of log reports mentioned them, year after year.

The Army finally found a way to close the road without admitting the real reason for the closure. The construction of Michie Stadium in 1924, followed shortly by the extension of the housing area of Connor Loop, effectively chopped the road up so that only short sections of it remained which were unusable for any practical reasons. An official memorandum closed the road to any vehicular or animal traffic for good in 1925. The reason stated was *safety* but the real reason was an incident that involved one of the school's new trucks in its fledgling automotive fleet.

An ambitious cadet squad leader had been directed to take his cadets on a ruck march up the hill. As cadets have been known to do, he decided to look for an easier solution to the task. Since he had access to the vehicle, he thought that he could use the short section of the road between Delafield Pond and Connor Loop to get his squad halfway up the hill and then walk from there. He loaded up his cadets and took off on the route past the fatal curve in the road. What he reported was the same thing that had been reported literally hundreds of times before.

Out of the morning mist appeared a horse-drawn carriage hurtling down the road. Suddenly, several men appeared on the hill above the road dressed in clothing that was fifty years out of date and firing rifles that were just as antiquated. The driver and a passenger on the front of the carriage were both thrown from the carriage. The carriage itself plummeted over the edge of the road while the horses galloped away in their broken gear. The entire time, not a single sound was heard.

The truck swerved and screeched to a halt only inches away from the prostrate form of the stage driver and dangerously close to going over the edge of the road themselves. Cadets leapt out of the truck and rushed to offer aid without thinking about how odd the event was. When they arrived at the front of the truck, the stage driver was gone. Those who rushed to aid anyone who might have been in the carriage reported that the carriage had also disappeared, leaving no trace that it had ever been there. Several of the cadets reacted to the threat that was perceived from the bandits that had been attacking from the hill but these too had gone. Confused, the cadets returned to their ruck march, but reported the incident when they got back that evening. The cadet squad leader who had borrowed the truck was disciplined, but no further action was taken.

This near-fatal ghost collision was the real reason for the permanent closure of the road. So, actually, it did have something to do with safety, just not in the way that the base stated in the memo.

The road itself can still be seen in those places where it has not been built or paved over. It can be accessed from a path behind Delafield Pond and is still traversable for about a mile of its length. Rarely are stories heard about the phantom stage these days, but then rarely does anyone travel this road anymore. Still, more than a few hikers and hunters have reported that strange, silent sight. A treasure hunter or two, searching for the missing boxes of gold and silver, have also been frightened off of the hillside and have given up their search for material gain due to witnessing the continuing struggle of the bandits to obtain the silver and gold and the fatally flawed attempt by the guards to protect their charge.

The section where the attack occurred lies about sixty feet above the current Merritt Road, slightly north of the Catholic Chapel. The stone wall over which the stage plummeted can in fact still be seen if you look through the trees and up the hill. In the autumn, when the trees are bare, it is quite visible, standing out against the hillside like stubborn bones that refuse to stay buried.

Conclusion

These are only thirteen of the many stories involving the ghosts of West Point. We have alluded to others such as the ghost of Viele in the cemetery or the ghost of the laborer who was killed while constructing the train tunnel under The Plain. There is also the legend of the Ghost Boatman of Lusk Reservoir that does nothing more menacing than float silently across the lake on clear moonlit nights. There are many sightings of cadets in period uniforms floating with only their heads and shoulders above the ground in the central cadet area. This area has been built up over and over again over the years, and the belief is that the ghost of the cadets past are still marching on their parade surface which is now four feet below ground. The most famous West Point ghost is probably the ghost of the Lost Fifties. In a room that is now used as a storage area, many cadets have reported a ghostly presence, biting cold, and a crushing pressure on their chests. An entire novel has been written about this particular apparition.

Other notable spirits include former professors, both malignant and benign. At least two animal ghosts are topics of conversation, a horse that causes havoc in classes that are now held in the converted remains of what was once the largest indoor riding hall on the east coast, and a floating squirrel that at this time has no story behind it which I can discover, but apparently has been seen on at least a few occasions. There are soldiers who return in death to haunt the halls where they once lived and studied. There was even once a large prisoner of war camp on the grounds that held German POWs. At least one violently unrepentant Nazi has terrorized cadets at the site of the former camp. The old enlisted hospital between the New Brick and Lee housing areas is home to spirits that keep normally curious and possibly delinquent children well outside its dark halls. A rather reliable spirit is the cadet that often appears in mid-nineteenth century garb to the CQ (Charge of Quarters) and reports that "All is clear," and then vanishes.

West Point is the oldest continuously manned military base in the country, and as such, will never want for tales that defy the logic and reason that is taught within its walls. I began this study as a skeptic. To date, I remain skeptical but am certainly a bit more apprehensive when I wind up working late in my office. The place lends itself to odd sounds and echoes. Before, I had an explanation for all of these shadows and echoes. Now…perhaps my explanation is stated with a bit less finality than it was before.

I thank you for your indulgence in reading my tales. I hope that at the least they entertained. Perhaps they allowed you for just a moment to indulge the "what if…" inside all of us. At best, I would extend to you the offer that West Point extends to all seekers of knowledge. Come visit us. Walk the halls. Stroll the cemetery. Stand on the Plain. And listen.

Perhaps you will hear a sound that is nothing more than a breeze or see a change in light that is nothing more than the shadow of the leaves on the ground. Or perhaps you will find yourself with no explanation other than the spirits of those who have passed this way before you. Either way, we hope to see you soon.

~Major Thad Krasnesky